I0429048

"Curiosity is the most powerful thing you own"

James Cameron

100 Quotes Regarding Success

Success is the achievement of a goal, a victory versus a competitor, a victory versus a previous time or distance or some other measurable mark. An accomplishment of some sort. It is the attainment of a higher social status. It is the opposite of failure. It is self defined in some areas such as that of relationships, raising children, and life in general. There are many definitions for success however I have chosen quotes that inspire and touch on the subject that I feel comes with the territory and can be used to gain insight and/or inspire motivation.

And I Quote... Success

Herman Melville observed Thomas Edison day after day tinkering unsuccessfully for weeks on end before interrupting **"It is better to fail in originality than to succeed in imitation."** Edison kept at his work not missing a beat **"I have not failed. I've just found 10,000 ways that won't work."**

1. Failure is the condiment that gives success its flavor. *~Truman Capote*

2. Don't let what you cannot do interfere with what you can do. *~John R. Wooden*

3. Motivation is what gets you started. Habit is what keeps you going. *~Jim Ryun*

4. Fortune sides with him who dares. *~Virgil*

5. All our dreams can come true if we have the courage to pursue them. ~*Walt Disney*

6. Failure defeats losers, failure inspires winners. ~*Robert T. Kiyosaki*

7. Every day I get up and look through the Forbes list of the richest people in America. If I'm not there, I go to work. ~*Vinnie Rege*

8. Good things come to people who wait, but better things come to those who go out and get them. ~*Anonymous*

9. If you do what you always did, you will get what you always got. ~*Anonymous*

10. Success is walking from failure to failure with no loss of enthusiasm. ~*Winston Churchill*

11. Just when the caterpillar thought the world was ending, he turned into a butterfly. ~*Proverb*

12. Successful entrepreneurs are givers and not takers of positive energy. ~*Anonymous*

13. You live longer once you realize that any time spent being unhappy is wasted. ~*Ruth Renkl*

14. Let no feeling of discouragement prey upon you, and in the end you are sure to succeed. ~*Abraham Lincoln*

15. Try not to become a person of success, but rather try to become a person of value. ~*Albert Einstein*

16. Poor people have a big TV. Rich people have a big library. ~*Jim Rohn*

17. I have not failed. I've just found 10,000 ways that won't work. ~*Thomas A. Edison*

18. Success is a magnet that draws many followers ~*Edward Counsel*

19. A successful man is one who can lay a firm foundation with the bricks others have thrown at him. ~*David Brinkley*

20. All you need in this life is ignorance and confidence; then success is sure. ~*Mark Twain*

21. The whole secret of a successful life is to find out what is one's destiny to do, and then do it. ~*Henry Ford*

22. If you're going through hell keep going. ~*Winston Churchill*

23. The ones who are crazy enough to think they can change the world, are the ones that do. ~*Anonymous*

24. Don't raise your voice, improve your argument. ~*Anonymous*

25. Learn everything you can, anytime you can, from anyone you can - there will always come a time when you will be grateful you did. *~Sarah Caldwell*

26. The meaning of life is to find your gift. The purpose of life is to give it away. *~Anonymous*

27. The distance between insanity and genius is measured only by success. *~Bruce Feirstein*

28. When you stop chasing the wrong things you give the right things a chance to catch you. *~Lolly Daskal*

29. Don't be afraid to give up the good to go for the great. *~John D. Rockefeller*

30. No masterpiece was ever created by a lazy artist.*~ Anonymous*

31. Coming together is a beginning; keeping together is progress; working together is success. *~Henry Ford*

32. The road to success for 99% of people isn't a jump! It's a steady incline from one successful project to the next. *~Lee Morris*

33. Choice, not circumstances, determines your success. *~Anonymous*

34. Do one thing every day that scares you. *~Anonymous*

35. What's the point of being alive if you don't at least try to do something remarkable. *~Anonymous*

36. Life is not about finding yourself. Life is about creating yourself. *~Lolly Daskal*

37. Nothing in the world is more common than unsuccessful people with talent. *~Anonymous*

38. A man can be as great as he wants to be. If you believe in yourself and have the courage, the determination, the dedication, the competitive drive and if you are willing to sacrifice the little things in life and pay the price for the things that are worthwhile, it can be done. *~Vince Lombardi*

39. Your problem isn't the problem. Your reaction is the problem. *~Anonymous*

40. You can do anything, but not everything. *~Anonymous*

41. Success seems to be connected with action. Successful people keep moving. They make mistakes but they don't quit. *~Conrad Hilton*

42. There are two types of people who will tell you that you cannot make a difference in this world: those who are afraid to try and those who are afraid you will succeed. *~Ray Goforth*

43. Thinking should become your capital asset, no matter whatever ups and downs you come across in your life. *~Dr. APJ Kalam*

44. I find that the harder I work, the more luck I seem to have. *~Thomas Jefferson*

45. The starting point of all achievement is desire. *~Napolean Hill*

46. Success is the sum of small efforts, repeated day-in and day-out. *~Robert Collier*

47. Obstacles are those frightful things you see when you take your eyes off the goal. *~Henry Ford*

48. All progress takes place outside the comfort zone. *~Michael John Bobak*

49. You may only succeed if you desire succeeding; you may only fail if you do not mind failing. *~Philippos*

50. Courage is resistance to fear, mastery of fear - not absence of fear. *~Mark Twain*

51. Only put off until tomorrow what you are willing to die having left undone. *~Pablo Picasso*

52. People often say that motivation doesn't last. Well, neither does

bathing - that's why we recommend it daily. *~Zig Ziglar*

53. We become what we think about most of the time, and that's the strangest secret. *~Earl Nightingale*

54. The only place where success comes before work is in the dictionary. *~Vidal Sassoon*

55. A minute's success pays the failures of years. *~Robert Browning*

56. I find that when you have a real interest in life and a curious life, that sleep is not the most important thing. *~Martha Stewart*

57. It's not what you look at that matters, it's what you see. *~Anonymous*

58. The road to success and the road to failure are almost exactly the same. *~Colin R. Davis*

59. To have success, you can't let failure stop you. To have great success, you can't let success stop you. *~Robert Brault*

60. Success is liking yourself, liking what you do, and liking how you do it. *~Maya Angelou*

61. If at first you don't succeed, you're running about average. *~M.H. Alderson*

62. Some people dream of success... while others wake up and work hard at it. ~*Author Unknown*

63. The first step toward success is taken when you refuse to be a captive of the environment in which you first find yourself. ~*Mark Caine*

64. People who succeed have momentum. The more they succeed, the more they want to succeed, and the more they find a way to succeed. Similarly, when someone is failing, the tendency is to get on a downward spiral that can even become a self-fulfilling prophecy. ~*Tony Robbins*

65. When I dare to be powerful - to use my strength in the service of my vision, then it becomes less and less important whether I am afraid. ~*Audre Lorde*

66. There is only one success — to be able to spend your life in your own way. ~*Christopher Morley*

67. The successful warrior is the average man, with laser-like focus. ~*Bruce Lee*

68. Take up one idea. Make that one idea your life -- think of it, dream of it, live on that idea. Let the brain, muscles, nerves, every part of your body, be full of that idea, and just leave every other idea alone. This is the way to success. ~*Swami Vivekananda*

69. Develop success from failures. Discouragement and failure are

two of the surest stepping stones to success. ~*Dale Carnegie*

70. If you don't design your own life plan, chances are you'll fall into someone else's plan. And guess what they have planned for you? Not much. ~ *Jim Rohn*

71. If you genuinely want something, don't wait for it -- teach yourself to be impatient. ~*Gurbaksh Chahal*

72. Don't let the fear of losing be greater than the excitement of winning. ~*Robert Kiyosaki*

73. If you want to make a permanent change, stop focusing on the size of your problems and start focusing on the size of you! ~*T. Harv Eker*

74. Success is the child of audacity. ~*Benjamin Disraeli*

75. Successful people do what unsuccessful people are not willing to do. Don't wish it were easier, wish you were better. ~*Jim Rohn*

76. The number one reason people fail in life is because they listen to their friends, family, and neighbors. ~*Napoleon Hill*

77. The reason most people never reach their goals is that they don't define them, or ever seriously consider them as believable or achievable. Winners can tell you where they are going, what they plan to do along the way, and who will be sharing the adventure with them. ~*Denis Watiley*

78. In my experience, there is only one motivation, and that is desire. No reasons or principle contain it or stand against it. *~Jane Smiley*

79. Success does not consist in never making mistakes but in never making the same one a second time. *~George Bernard Shaw*

80. I don't want to get to the end of my life and find that I lived just the length of it. I want to have lived the width of it as well. *~Diane Ackerman*

81. You must expect great things of yourself before you can do them. *~Michael Jordan*

82. A goal is a dream with a deadline. *~Napoleon Hill*

83. People rarely succeed unless they have fun in what they are doing. *~Dale Carnegie*

84. There is no chance, no destiny, no fate, that can hinder or control the firm resolve of a determined soul. *~Ella Wheeler Wilcox*

85. Our greatest fear should not be of failure but of succeeding at things in life that don't really matter. *~Francis Chan*

86. You've got to get up every morning with determination if you're going to go to bed with satisfaction. *~George Lorimer*

87. To be successful you must accept all challenges that come your

way. You can't just accept the ones you like. ~*Mike Gafka*

88. Success is...knowing your purpose in life, growing to reach your maximum potential, and sowing seeds that benefit others. ~ *John C. Maxwell*

89. Be miserable. Or motivate yourself. Whatever has to be done, it's always your choice. ~*Wayne Dyer*

90. To accomplish great things, we must not only act, but also dream, not only plan, but also believe.~ *Anatole France*

91. Most of the important things in the world have been accomplished by people who have kept on trying when there seemed to be no help at all. ~*Dale Carnegie*

92. You measure the size of the accomplishment by the obstacles you had to overcome to reach your goals. ~*Booker T. Washington*

93. Real difficulties can be overcome; it is only the imaginary ones that are unconquerable. ~*Theodore N. Vail*

94. It is better to fail in originality than to succeed in imitation. ~*Herman Melville*

95. Take up one idea. Make that one idea your life - think of it, dream of it, live on that idea. Let the brain, muscles, nerves, every part of your body, be full of that idea, and just leave every other idea alone. This is the way to success. ~*Swami Vivekananda*

96. Help others achieve their dreams and you will achieve yours. *~Les Brown*

97. If you want to achieve greatness stop asking for permission. *~Anonymous*

98. Things work out best for those who make the best of how things work out. *~John Wooden*

99. You may have to fight a battle more than once to win it. *~Margaret Thatcher*

100. You can't connect the dots looking forward; you can only connect them looking backwards. So you have to trust that the dots will somehow connect in your future. You have to trust in something - your gut, destiny, life, karma, whatever. This approach has never let me down, and it has made all the difference in my life. *~Steve Jobs*

Quotes for Inspiration

And I Quote... Inspiration

Pablo Picasso had his canvas before him. He swapped one of his many brushes out and mixed different shades of paints together, prepping his canvas, eyeing up his subjects, again he mixed a few more paints together when Napoleon Bonaparte who was watching him toiling from afar made his way hastily over to the artist **"Over-preparation is the foe of inspiration"** Pablo went about laying the backdrop on his canvas ignoring the short, squat man behind him. Napoleon irked by the lack of response repeated **"Over-preparation is the foe of inspiration."** Ben Franklin overhearing the stunted gentleman said pardon me sir but **"By failing to prepare, you are preparing to fail."** After Ben had put in his two cents Picasso stood up and taped off the left side of the canvas and spoke **"Inspiration exists, but it has to find you working"** now please accept my apologies in advance as I overlook you and your comments. Haha Picasso chuckled, overlook you.

I've missed more than 9000 shots in my career. I've lost almost 300 games. 26 times I've been trusted to take the game winning shot and missed. I've failed over and over and over again in my life. And that is why I succeed. ~Michael Jordan

You miss 100% of the shots you don't take. *~Wayne Gretzky*

Every strike brings me closer to the next home run. *~Babe Ruth*

Whatever the mind of man can conceive and believe, it can achieve. *~Napoleon Hill*

The mind is everything. What you think you become. *~Buddha*

Winning isn't everything, but wanting to win is. *~Vince Lombardi*

You can never cross the ocean until you have the courage to lose sight of the shore. *~Christopher Columbus*

Whether you think you can or you think you can't, you're right.

~Henry Ford

People often say that motivation doesn't last. Well, neither does bathing. That's why we recommend it daily. *~Zig Ziglar*

Never put off till tomorrow what you can do today. *~Thomas Jefferson*

Success doesn't come to you, you go to it. *~Marva Collins*

Never tell me the sky's the limit when there are footprints on the moon. *~Author Unknown*

It is never too late to be what you might have been. *~George Eliot*

What lies behind us and what lies before us are tiny matters compared to what lies within us. *~Ralph Waldo Emerson*

The more I want to get something done, the less I call it work. *~Richard Bach*

An obstacle is often a stepping stone. *~Prescott*

Do not go where the path may lead, go instead where there is no path and leave a trail. *~Ralph Waldo Emerson*

By failing to prepare, you are preparing to fail. *~Benjamin Franklin*

The journey of a thousand miles begins with one step. *~Lao Tzu*

What counts is not necessarily the size of the dog in the fight – it's the size of the fight in the dog. *~Dwight D. Eisenhower*

Quotes on Forgiveness

The whole world may forgive you but the hardest thing in life is to forgive yourself *~Richard Briggs*

Forgive, forget. Bear with the faults of others as you would have them bear with yours. *~Phillips Brooks*

Forgiveness is not always easy. At times, it feels more painful than the wound we suffered, to forgive the one that inflicted it. And yet, there is no peace without forgiveness. *~Marianne Williams*

Forgiveness is the final form of love *~Reinhold Niebhur*

It's one of the greatest gifts you can give yourself, to forgive. Forgive everybody. *~Maya Angelou*

The weak can never forgive. Forgiveness is the attribute of the strong. *~Mahatma Gandhi*

Most of us can forgive and forget; we just don't want the other person to forget that we forgave. *~Ivern Ball*

When you hold resentment toward another, you are bound to that person or condition by an emotional link that is stronger than steel. Forgiveness is the only way to dissolve that link and get free. *~Catherine Ponder*

True forgiveness is when you can say, "Thank you for that experience." *~Oprah Winfrey*

Forgiveness is the fragrance that the violet sheds on the heel that has crushed it. *~Mark Twain*

To be wronged is nothing, unless you continue to remember it. *~Confucius*

Quotes of Encouragement

Nothing is particularly hard if you divide it into small jobs. *~Henry Ford*

The fear of suffering is worse than the suffering itself. *~Paulo Coehlo*

There is no failure. Only feedback. *~Robert Allen*

I believe that anyone can conquer fear by doing the things he fears to do, provided he keeps doing them until he gets a record of successful experiences behind him. *~Eleanor Roosevelt*

Mistakes are the portals of discovery. *~James Joyce*

Your mind will answer most questions if you learn to relax and wait for the answer. *~William S Burroughs*

Most fears are just illusions. *~Gary Null*

Every thought is a seed. If you plant crab apples don't count on harvesting Golden Delicious. *~Bill Meyer*

When you feel like giving up. Remember why you held on for so long in the first place. *~Unknown*

What the caterpillar calls the end of the world, the master calls a butterfly. *~Richard Bach*

I have heard there are troubles of more than one kind.
Some come from ahead and some come from behind.

But I've bought a big bat. I'm all ready you see.
Now my troubles are going to have troubles with me! *~Dr. Seuss*

When written in Chinese the word "crisis" is composed of two characters one represents danger and the other represents opportunity. *~John F Kennedy*

A word of encouragement during a failure is worth more than an hour of praise after success. *~Unknown*

Every failure is a step closer to success. *~Unknown*

Courage doesn't always roar. Sometimes courage is the little voice at the end of the day that says I'll try again tomorrow. *~Mary Anne Radmacher*

Hardship often prepares an ordinary person for an extraordinary destiny. *~C.S. Lewis*

Never never never never never give up. *~Winston Churchill*

Every artist was first an amateur. *~Ralph Waldo Emerson*

The important thing is not being afraid to take a chance. Remember, the greatest failure is to not try. Once you find something you love to do, be the best at doing it. *~Debbi Fields*

In response to those who say to stop dreaming and face reality, I say keep dreaming and make reality. *~Kristian Kan*

Quotes of Wisdom

Wisdom is the ability to think and act using knowledge, experience, understanding, common sense, and insight. Wisdom has been regarded as one of four cardinal virtues; and as a virtue, it is a habit or disposition to perform the action with the highest degree of adequacy under any given circumstance. This implies a possession of knowledge or the seeking thereof to apply it to the given circumstance. This involves an understanding of people, objects, events, situations, and the willingness as well as the ability to apply perception, judgement, and action in keeping with the understanding of what is the optimal course of action. It often requires control of one's emotional reactions (the passions) so that the universal principle of reason prevails to determine one's action. In short, wisdom is a disposition to find the truth coupled with an optimum judgement as to what actions should be taken to deliver the correct outcome.

And I Quote…. WISDOM

The cards had been dealt, Aesop looked at his pocket cards, looked at the flop and folded. He glanced at those seated at the table and grinned **"Appearances are often deceiving"**
St. Augustine looked at his pocket cards and tossed them towards the center of the table, mucking his hand **"Patience is the companion of wisdom".** On their way towards the middle of the table one of the cards flipped over to reveal the Jack of Spades. John Kennedy, the dealer, showed the card to all players and warned **"The greater our knowledge increases the more our ignorance unfolds"** play continued to the left where Ed Norton raised the pot ten fold in a reserved manner **"Life, like poker has an element of risk. It shouldn't be avoided. It should be faced."** Oliver Wendell Holmes Sr stared long and hard at Norton, examining his body language and reading his tell and calling his bluff. He eyed up the amount Norton had raised and pushed his stack all in **"The young man knows the rules, but the old man knows the exceptions"**

The art of being wise is the art of knowing what to overlook. ~*William James*

The only true wisdom is in knowing you know nothing. ~*Socrates*

It's not what you look at that matters, It's what you see. ~*Henry David Thoreau*

A day of worry is more exhausting than a week of work. ~*John Lubbock*

Beware of false knowledge; it is more dangerous than ignorance. ~*George Bernard Shaw*

Everything that irritates us about others can lead us to an understanding of ourselves. ~*Carl Jung*

Knowing others is wisdom, knowing yourself is enlightenment. ~*Lao Tzu*

It requires wisdom to understand wisdom: the music is nothing if the audience is deaf. ~*Walter Lippman*

If you call failures experiments, you can put them in your resume and claim them as achievements. ~*Mason Cooley*

The smallest deed is greater than the greatest intention. ~*John Burroughs*

The superior man blames himself. The inferior man blames others. ~*Don Shula*

Please all and you will please none. ~*Aesop*

Suffering is one of life's great teachers. ~*Bryant H McGill*

Turn your wounds into wisdom. ~*Oprah Winfrey*

Kindness is more important than wisdom, and the recognition of this is the beginning of wisdom. ~*Theodore Isaac Rubin*

Wisdom consists of the anticipation of consequences. ~*Norman Cousins*

The seeds of wisdom are watered through the art of observation. ~*Robert McGinley*

Knowledge is of no value unless you put it into practice. ~*Anton Chekhov*

Preconceived notions are the locks on the door to wisdom. ~*Mary Browne*

Wisdom is the reward you get for a lifetime of listening when you'd have preferred to talk. ~*Doug Larson*

The wisdom of the sage absorbs the actions of fools ~*Robert McGinley*

Quotes regarding Truth

The wealthiest truth in life, of all that there may be, is that the only things of value cost nothing…they're free. *~Daniel Shelley*

Three things cannot be long hidden, the sun, the moon, and the truth. *~Buddha*

Everything we hear is an opinion, not a fact. Everything we see is a perspective, not the truth. *~Marcus Aurelius*

Do not mistake probability for truth, for it is a notorious liar. *~Robert Brault*

There is no truth. There is only perception. *~Gustave Flaubert*

Honesty is the first chapter in the book of wisdom *~Thomas Jefferson*

I'm for truth, no matter who tells it. I'm for justice, no matter who it's for or against. *~Malcolm X*

If you tell the truth you won't have to remember anything. *~Mark Twain*

There is nothing more deceptive than an obvious fact. *~Sir Arthur Conan Doyle*

A lot of truth is said in jest. *~Marshall Mathers*

Never apologize for showing feeling. When you do so, you apologize for the truth. *~Benjamin Disraeli*

Your problem is how you are going to spend this one odd and precious life you have been issued. Whether you're going to spend it trying to look good and creating the illusion that you have power over people and circumstances, or whether you are going to taste it, enjoy it and find out the truth about who you are. *~Anne Lamott*

It's no wonder that truth is stranger than fiction. Fiction has to make sense. *~Mark Twain*

The truth is incontrovertible. Malice may attack it, ignorance may deride it, but in the end, there it is. *~Winston Churchill*

Quotes regarding Focus

And I Quote...Focus

Einstein scratched his head staring at his equation on the blackboard, he rubbed his forefinger and thumb on opposite sides of his chin in a pondering motion **"I used to go away for weeks in a state of confusion."** Alexander Graham Bell patted Albert on the back **"Concentrate all your thoughts upon the work at hand. The sun's rays do not burn until brought to a focus."**

The key to success is to focus our conscious mind on things we desire not things we fear. *~Brian Tracy*

Realize deeply that the present moment is all you ever have. Make the now the primary focus of your life. *~Eckhart Tolle*

Concentrate all your thoughts upon the work at hand. The sun's rays do not burn until brought to a focus. *~Alexander Graham Bell*

If you just focus on the smallest details, you never get the big picture right. *~Leroy Hood*

One reason so few of us achieve what we truly want is that we never direct our focus; we never concentrate our power. Most people dabble their way through life, never deciding to master anything in particular. *~Tony Robbins*

The earlier you learn that you should focus on what you have, and not obsess about what you don't have, the happier you will be. *~Amy Poehler*

Don't dwell on what went wrong. Instead, focus on what to do next. Spend your energies on moving forward toward finding the answer. *~Denis Waitley*

A clear vision, backed by definite plans, gives you a tremendous feeling of confidence and personal power. *~Brian Tracy*

I don't care how much power, brilliance or energy you have, if you don't harness it and focus it on a specific target, and hold it there you're never going to accomplish as much as your ability warrants. *~Zig Ziglar*

All that we are is the result of what we have thought. *~Buddha*

Energy is the essence of life. Every day you decide how you're going to use it by knowing what you want and what it takes to reach that goal, and by maintaining focus. *~Oprah Winfrey*

Visualize this thing you want. See it, feel it, believe in it. Make your mental blueprint and begin. *~Robert Collier*

To conquer frustration, one must remain intensely focused on the outcome, not the obstacles. *~T.F. Hodge*

Most people have no idea of the giant capacity we can immediately command when we focus all of our resources on mastering a single area of our lives. *~Tony Robbins*

Instead of focusing on how much you can accomplish, focus on how much you can absolutely love what you're doing. *~Leo Babauta*

Successful people maintain a positive focus in life no matter what is going on around them. They stay focused on their past successes rather than their past failures, and on the next action steps they need to take to get them closer to the fulfillment of their goals rather than all the other distractions that life presents to them. ~*Jack Canfield*

We focus so much on our differences, and that is creating, I think, a lot of chaos and negativity and bullying in the world. And I think if everybody focused on what we all have in common - which is - we all want to be happy. ~*Ellen Degeneres*

Quotes and Leadership

Not the cry, but the flight of a wild duck, leads the flock to fly and follow. ~*Chinese Proverb*

Leadership: The art of getting someone else to do something you want done because he wants to do it. ~*Dwight D Eisenhower*

The art of leadership is saying no, not yes. It is very easy to say yes. ~*Tony Blair*

The people follow the example of those above them. ~*Chinese Proverb*

A leader is best when people barely know he exists, when his work is done, his aim fulfilled, they will say: we did it ourselves. ~*Lao Tzu*

Leadership is the capacity to translate vision into reality. ~*Warren Bennis*

Leadership is lifting a person's vision to high sights, the raising of a person's performance to a higher standard, the building of a personality beyond its normal limitations. ~*Peter Drucker*

I start with the premise that the function of leadership is to produce more leaders, not more followers. ~*Ralph Nader*

Leadership is influence. ~*John C. Maxwell*

People buy into the leader before they buy into the vision. ~*John Maxwell*

The key to successful leadership today is influence, not authority. ~*Kenneth Blanchard*

A great leader's courage to fulfill his vision comes from passion, not position. ~*John Maxwell*

A true leader has the confidence to stand alone, the courage to make tough decisions, and the compassion to listen to the needs of others. He does not set out to be a leader, but becomes one by the equality of his actions and the integrity of his intent. *~Douglas MacArthur*

If your actions inspire others to dream more, learn more, do more and become more, you are a leader. *~John Quincy Adams*

The function of leadership is to produce more leaders, not more followers. *~Ralph Nader*

Quotes on Friendship

And I Quote…. Friendship

Lucius Annaeus Seneca looked at her companions, giving each a soft gaze **"One of the most beautiful qualities of true friendship is to understand and to be understood."** She walked over and hugged each of them, one by one. Hubert Humphrey smiled back at Lucius after hugging **"The greatest gift of life is friendship, and I have received it."** After Marcel Proust exchanged a warm embrace, he stared back at Lucius then turned to the others **"Let us be grateful to people who make us happy, they are the charming gardeners who make our souls blossom."** Ralph Waldo Emerson in turn also took the time to hug each in the group **"The only way to have a friend is to be one"**

There comes a point in your life when you realize who really matters, who never did, and who always will. *~Anonymous*

A friend is someone who can see the truth and pain in you even when you are fooling everyone else. *~Anonymous*

If you're alone, I'll be your shadow. If you want to cry, I'll be your shoulder. If you want a hug, I'll be your pillow. If you need to be happy, I'll be your smile... But anytime you need a friend, I'll just be me. *~Anonymous*

Walking with a friend in the dark is better than walking alone in the light. *~Helen Keller*

Let us be grateful to people who make us happy, they are the charming gardeners who make our souls blossom. *~Marcel Proust*

The language of friendship is not words but meanings. *~Henry*

30

David Thoreau

A friend is a gift you give yourself. *~Robert Louis Stevenson*

Where would you be without friends? The people to pick you up when you need lifting? We come from homes far from perfect, so you end up almost parent and sibling to your friends - your own chosen family. There's nothing like a really loyal, dependable, good friend. Nothing. *~Jennifer Aniston*

There is some self-interest behind every friendship. There is no friendship without self-interests. This is a bitter truth. *~Chanakya*

A man's friendships are one of the best measures of his worth. *~Charles Darwin*

Never explain - your friends do not need it and your enemies will not believe you anyway. *~Elbert Hubbard*

I have friends in overalls whose friendship I would not swap for the favor of the kings of the world. *~Thomas Edison*

Quotes about Patience

Patience is the ability to count down before you blast off. *~Author Unknown*

A handful of patience is worth more than a bushel of brains. *~Dutch Proverb*

Genius is nothing but a great aptitude for patience. *~George-Louis de Buffon*

Adopt the pace of nature: her secret is patience. *~Ralph Waldo Emerson*

Patience and perseverance have a magical effect before which difficulties disappear and obstacles vanish. *~John Quincy Adams*

Experience has taught me this, that we undo ourselves by impatience. Misfortunes have their life and their limits, their sickness and their health. *~Michel de Montaigne*

There is no road too long to the man who advances deliberately and without undue haste; there are no honors too distant to the man who prepares himself for them with patience. *~Jean De La Bruyare*

He that can have patience can have what he will. *~Benjamin Franklin*

Patience is bitter, but its fruit is sweet. *~Jean Jacques Rousseau*

Patience, persistence and perspiration make an unbeatable combination for success. *~Napoleon Hill*

Have patience with all things, But, first of all with yourself. *~Saint Francis de Sales*

Patience is not simply the ability to wait - it's how we behave while we're waiting. *~Joyce Meyer*

Never cut a tree down in the wintertime. Never make a negative decision in the low time. Never make your most important decisions when you are in your worst moods. Wait. Be patient. The storm will pass. The spring will come. *~Robert H. Schuller*

Patience and wisdom walk hand in hand, like two one-armed lovers.*~Jarod Kintz*

Work hard. And have patience. Because no matter who you are, you're going to get hurt in your career and you have to be patient to get through the injuries. *~Randy Johnson*

The strongest of all warriors are these two—Time and Patience. *~Leo Tolstoy*

Our real blessings often appear to us in the shape of pains, losses and disappointments; but let us have patience and we soon shall see them in their proper figures. *~Joseph Addison*

Genius is eternal patience. *~Michelangelo*

Patience and diligence, like faith, remove mountains. *~William Penn*

Patience is the art of concealing your impatience. *~Guy Kawasaki*

Quotes of Advice

Hearses don't have luggage racks. Stay Humble. *~Jenny Griffin*

Get Involved! *~Ralph Alesia*

If you can't love something accept it, if you can't accept it, leave it. Life is about choice. *~Jenny Griffin*

And I Quote…. DEATH

The four of them had gathered at the graveyard. Leonardo Da Vinci stared out at all the tombstones **"While I thought that I was learning how to live, I have been learning how to die."** Marcus Tullius Cicero knelt down and placed a rose on the grave before him
"The life of the dead is placed in the memory of the living" Edgar Allen Poe pondered a moment and thought aloud **"The boundaries which divide life from death are at best shadowy and vague. Who shall say where the one ends and the other begins?"** Woody Allen concluded **"I am not afraid of death, I just don't wanna be there when it happens"**

If the afterlife is so wonderful why is the reaper so grim? *~Anonymous*

Your stroll through the tunnel of life ends with a train named death. *~Robert McGinley*

Nothing is as welcome as the next breath *~Hal Deal*

The fear of death follows from the fear of life. A man who lives fully is prepared to die at any time. *~Mark Twain*

He who doesn't fear death dies only once. *~Giovanni Falcone*

If man were immortal he could be perfectly sure of seeing the day when everything in which he had trusted should betray his trust, and, in short, of coming eventually to hopeless misery. He would break down, at last, as every good fortune, as every dynasty, as every civilization does. In place of this we have death. *~Charles*

Sanders Peirce

People do not die for us immediately, but remain bathed in a sort of aura of life which bears no relation to true immortality but through which they continue to occupy our thoughts in the same way as when they were alive. It is as though they were traveling abroad. *~Marcel Proust*

Death is not the greatest loss in life. The greatest loss is what dies inside us while we live. *~Norman Cousins*

Quotes on Ignorance

Beware of false knowledge; it is more dangerous than ignorance. ~*George Bernard Shaw*

My mother said I must always be intolerant of ignorance but understanding of illiteracy. That some people, unable to go to school, were more educated and more intelligent than college professors. ~*Maya Angelou*

Nothing in all the world is more dangerous than sincere ignorance and conscientious stupidity. ~*Martin Luther King Jr.*

Ignorance is the curse of God; knowledge is the wing wherewith we fly to heaven. ~*William Shakespeare*

Real knowledge is to know the extent of one's ignorance. ~*Confucius*

Anyway, no drug, not even alcohol, causes the fundamental ills of society. If we're looking for the source of our troubles, we shouldn't test people for drugs, we should test them for stupidity, ignorance, greed and love of power. ~*P.J. O'Rourke*

Quotes on Work

If it was fun it wouldn't be called work! *~Anthony Marino*

Nothing is work unless you'd rather be doing something else. *~George Halas*

Opportunity is missed by most people because it is dressed in overalls and looks like work. *~Thomas Edison*

The supreme accomplishment is to blur the line between work and play. *~Arnold J Toynbee*

Sharpening Curiosity

Curiosity is the most powerful thing you own ~*James Cameron*

He who asks is a fool for five minutes, but he who does not ask remains a fool forever. ~*Chinese proverb*

Research is formalized curiosity. It is poking and prying with a purpose. ~*Zora Neale Hurston*

Quotes of War

And I Quote…. WAR

George Patton started the conversation **"The object of war is not to die for your country but to make the other bastard die for his."** Napoleon looked him up and down, nodding his head in a manner of agreement. **"You must not fight too often with one enemy, or you will teach him all your art of war."** Alexander the Great pushed the two to the side on his way towards the battle map **"I am not afraid of an army of lions led by a sheep; I am afraid of an army of sheep led by a lion."** Sun Tzu looked at the savage men, the brutes he thought.
"The supreme art of war is to subdue the enemy without fighting."

War does not determine who is right — only who is left. *~Bertrand Russell*

It'll be a great day when education gets all the money it wants and the Air Force has to hold a bake sale to buy bombers. *~Anonymous*

All the arms we need are for hugging. *~Anonymous*

Everyone's a pacifist between wars. It's like being a vegetarian between meals. *~Colman McCarthy*

The most persistent sound which reverberates through men's history is the beating of war drums. *~Arthur Koestler*

Never think that war, no matter how necessary, nor how justified, is not a crime. *~Ernest Hemingway*

I have no doubt that we will be successful in harnessing the sun's energy…. If sunbeams were weapons of war, we would have had solar energy centuries ago. *~Sir George Porter*

War would end if the dead could return. *~Stanley Baldwin*

Only the dead have seen the end of war. *~Plato*

War is the only game in which it doesn't pay to have the home-court advantage. *~Dick Motta*

Fighting for peace is like screwing for virginity. *~Anonymous*

All wars are civil wars, because all men are brothers. *~François Fénelon*

Quotes on Empathy

The great gift of human beings is that we have the power of empathy. *~Meryl Streep*

Empathy is the most radical of human emotions. *~Gloria Steinem*

If there is any one secret of success, it lies in the ability to get the other person's point of view and see things from his angle as well as your own. *~Henry Ford*

Empathy is about standing in someone else's shoes, feeling with his or her heart, seeing with his or her eyes. Not only is empathy hard to outsource and automate, but it makes the world a better place. *~Henry Pink*

The struggle of my life created empathy - I could relate to pain, being abandoned, having people not love me. *~Oprah Winfrey*

A prerequisite to empathy is simply paying attention to the person in pain. *~Daniel Goleman*

We need somebody who's got the heart, the empathy, to recognize what it's like to be a young teenage mom, the empathy to understand what it's like to be poor or African-American or gay or disabled or old - and that's the criterion by which I'll be selecting my judges. *~Barack Obama*

Sharpening Creativity

The author gathers words for his prose as a florist arranges flowers for their bouquet, selectively. *~Hal Deal*

The more you reason the less you create. *~Raymond Chandler*

10 of the Dumbest Quotes and 10 more by George W Bush

Is this chicken, what I have, or is this fish? I know it's tuna, but it says Chicken of the sea ~*Jessica Simpson*

How can mirrors be real if our eyes aren't real ~*Jaden Smith*

Whenever I watch TV and see those poor starving kids all over the world, I can't help but cry. I mean I'd love to be skinny like that but not with all those flies and death and stuff. ~*Mariah Carey*

I guess I'm gonna fade into Bolivian ~*Mike Tyson*

I've never really wanted to go to Japan simply because I do not like eating fish. And I know that's very popular out there in Africa ~*Britney Spears*

He speaks English, Spanish, and he's bilingual too ~*Don King*

If we don't succeed, we run the risk of failure ~*Dan Quayle*

I was asked to come to Chicago because Chicago is one of our fifty two states ~*Racquel Welch*

My sister's expecting a baby and I don't know whether I'm going to be an uncle or an aunt ~*Chuck Nevitt*

I want to rush for 1,000 or 1,500 yards, whatever comes first ~*George Rogers*

Rarely is the question asked 'Is our children learning?' ~*George W*

I think war is a dangerous place. ~*George W*

You know, one of the hardest parts of my job is to connect Iraq to the war on terror ~*George W*

For every fatal shooting, there were roughly three non-fatal shootings. And folks, this is unacceptable in America. It's just unacceptable. And we're going to do something about it. ~*George W*

People say, how can I help on this war against terror? How can I fight evil? You can do so by mentoring a child; by going into a shut-in's house and say I love you. ~*George W*

There's an old saying in Tennessee -- I know it's in Texas, probably in Tennessee -- that says, fool me once, shame on --shame on you. Fool me -- you can't get fooled again. ~*George W*

Too many good docs are getting out of the business. Too many OB-GYNs aren't able to practice their love with women all across this country. ~*George W*

Our enemies are innovative and resourceful, and so are we. They never stop thinking about new ways to harm our country and our people, and neither do we. ~*George W*

As yesterday's positive report card shows, childrens do learn when standards are high and results are measured. ~*George W*

Families is where our nation finds hope, where wings take dream. ~*George W*

Quotes on Stupidity

Two things are infinite: the universe and human stupidity; and I'm not sure about the universe. *~Albert Einstein*

If a cluttered desk is a sign of a cluttered mind, of what, then, is an empty desk a sign? *~Albert Einstein*

Never underestimate the power of stupid people in large groups. *~George Carlin*

Stupidity isn't punishable by death. If it was, there would be a hell of a population drop. *~Laurell K Hamilton*

I don't get high, but sometimes I wish I did. That way, when I messed up in life I would have an excuse. But right now there's no rehab for stupidity. *~Chris Rock*

You can't legislate against stupidity. *~Jesse Ventura*

Idleness is the stupidity of the body, and stupidity is the idleness of the mind. *~Johann G Seume*

Stupidity is an elemental force for which no earthquake is a match. *~Karl Kraus*

Quotes on Consequence

If you must ponder the price of consequence .. You cannot afford it. *~Weylin Caucci*

Hate is the consequence of fear; we fear something before we hate it; a child who fears noises becomes a man who hates noise. *~Cyril Connolly*

Happiness is not a reward - it is a consequence. Suffering is not a punishment - it is a result. *~Robert Green Ingersoll*

The disappearance of a sense of responsibility is the most far-reaching consequence of submission to authority. *~Stanley Milgram*

Productive achievement is a consequence and an expression of health and self-esteem, not its cause. *~Nathaniel Branden*

Success is a consequence and must not be a goal. *~Gustave Flaubert*

If you spend your time hoping someone will suffer the consequences for what they did to your heart, then you're allowing them to hurt you a second time in your mind. *~Shannon L Alder*

Acceptance of what has happened is the first step to overcoming the consequences of any misfortune. *~William James*

How much more grievous are the consequences of anger than the causes of it. *~Marcus Aurelius*

20 Quotes for Beer Lovers

He was a wise man, he who invented beer. *~Plato*

Beauty is in the eye of the beer holder. *~Kinky Friedman*

Beer is proof that God loves us and wants us to be happy. *~Ben Franklin*

Payday came and with it beer. *~Rudyard Kipling*

You can't be a real country unless you have a beer and an airline - it helps if you have some kind of football team, or some nuclear weapons, but in the very least you need a beer. *~Frank Zappa*

There are more old drunks than there are old doctors. *~Willie Nelson*

Beer makes you feel the way you ought to feel without beer. *~Henry Lawson*

When I read about the evils of drinking, I gave up reading. *~Henny Youngman*

A drunk man's words are a sober man's thoughts. *~Jena Legg*

Twenty-four hours in a day; twenty-four beers in a case. Coincidence? *~Stephen Wright*

A woman drove me to drink and I didn't even have the decency to thank her. *~W.C. Fields*

It takes only one drink to get me drunk. The trouble is, I can't remember if it's the thirteenth or the fourteenth. ~*George Burns*

I drink to make other people interesting. ~*George Jean Nathan*

I feel sorry for people who don't drink. When they wake up in the morning, that's as good as they're going to feel all day. ~*Frank Sinatra*

I drink when I have occasion, and sometimes when I have no occasion. ~*Miguel De Cervantes*

Drunk is feeling sophisticated when you can't say it. ~*Anonymous*

I'm Catholic and I can't commit suicide, but I plan to drink myself to death. ~*Jack Kerouac*

Well ya see, Norm, it's like this... A herd of buffalo can only move as fast as the slowest buffalo. And when the herd is hunted, it is the slowest and weakest ones at the back that are killed first. This natural selection is good for the herd as a whole, because the general speed and health of the whole group keeps improving by the regular killing of the weakest members. In much the same way, the human brain can only operate as fast as the slowest brain cells. Excessive intake of alcohol, as we know, kills brain cells. But naturally, it attacks the slowest and weakest brain cells first. In this way, regular consumption of beer eliminates the weaker brain cells, making the brain a faster and more efficient machine. That's why you always feel smarter after a few beers. ~*Cliff Claven*

A fine beer may be judged with only one sip, but it's better to be thoroughly sure. ~*Czech Proverb*

Sometimes when I reflect back on all the beer I drink I feel ashamed. Then I look into the glass and think about the workers in the brewery and all of their hopes and dreams. If I didn't drink this beer, they might be out of work and their dreams would be shattered. Then I say to myself, "It is better that I drink this beer and let their dreams come true than be selfish and worry about my liver. ~*Jack Handy*

There seems to be a direct correlation between the growth of muscle mass and perception of beauty to the ratio of alcohol consumption. ~*Robert McGinley*

20 Quotes to make you smile

When I die, I want to die like my grandfather who died peacefully in his sleep. Not screaming like all the passengers in his car. *~Will Rogers*

Politicians and diapers have one thing in common. They should both be changed regularly, and for the same reason. *~José Maria de Eça de Queiroz*

The only mystery in life is why the kamikaze pilots wore helmets *~Al McGuire*

The quickest way to double your money is to fold it over and put it back in your pocket. *~Will Rogers*

I couldn't repair your brakes so I made your horn louder. *~Steven Wright*

I asked God for a bike, but I know God doesn't work that way. So I stole a bike and asked for forgiveness. *~Emo Philips*

People who think they know everything are a great annoyance to those of us who do *~Isaac Asimov*

The early bird gets the worm, but the second mouse gets the cheese. *~Unknown*

Always borrow money from a pessimist. He won't expect it back. *~Oscar Wilde*

You are such a good friend that if we were on a sinking ship together and there was only one life jacket... I'd miss you heaps and think of you often. *~Anonymous*

If at first you don't succeed, skydiving is not for you! *~Henry Youngman*

If aliens are watching us through telescopes, they're going to think the dogs are the leaders of the planet. If you see two life forms, one of them's making a poop, the other one's carrying it for him, who would you assume is in charge? *~Jerry Seinfeld*

If women ran the world we wouldn't have wars, just intense negotiations every 28 days. *~Robin Williams*

Why do people keep running over a string a dozen times with their vacuum cleaner, then reach down, pick it up, examine it, then put it down to give their vacuum one more chance? *~Unknown*

Never go to a doctor whose office plants have died. *~Erma Bombeck*

At every party there are two kinds of people: those who want to go home and those who don't. The trouble is, they are usually married to each other. *~Ann Landers*

My therapist told me the way to achieve inner peace is to finish what I start. So far I've finished two bags of M&M's and a chocolate cake. I feel better already. *~Dave Barry*

Never, under any circumstances, take a sleeping pill and a laxative on the same night *~Dave Barry*

When tempted to fight fire with fire, remember that the fire department usually uses water. *~Anonymous*

The odds of going to the store for a loaf of bread and coming out with only a loaf of bread are three billion to one *~Erma Bombeck*

Quotes about Addiction

I have absolutely no pleasure in the stimulants in which I sometimes so madly indulge. It has not been in the pursuit of pleasure that I have periled life and reputation and reason. It has been the desperate attempt to escape from torturing memories, from a sense of insupportable loneliness and a dread of some strange impending doom. ~*Edgar Allen Poe*

We are addicted to our thoughts. We cannot change anything if we cannot change our thinking. ~*Santosh Kalwar*

I suspect it may be like the difference between a drinker and an alcoholic; the one merely reads books, the other needs books to make it through the day. ~*Gail Carriger*

Addiction is a serious disease; it will end with jail, mental institutions, or death. ~*Russell Brand*

If you are an approval addict, your behavior is as easy to control as that of any other junkie. All a manipulator need do is a simple two-step process: Give you what you crave, and then threaten to take it away. Every drug dealer in the world plays this game. ~*Harriet B. Braiker*

An over-indulgence of anything, even something as pure as water, can intoxicate. ~*Criss Jami*

This must be what an addict feels like, I think, trying to fight the pull of one last, quick read. My fingers itch toward the binding, and finally, with a sigh of regret, I just grab the book and open it, hungrily reading the story. ~*Jodi Picoult*

The priority of any addict is to anesthetize the pain of living to ease the passage of day with some purchased relief. *~Russell Brand*

This is what I think. Addiction is just a way of trying to get at something else. Something bigger. Call it transcendence if you want, but it's a fucked-up way, like a rat in a maze. We all want the same thing. We all have this hole. The thing you want offers relief, but it's a trap. *~Tess Callahan*

Quotes about devotion

I know the price of success: dedication, hard work, and an unremitting devotion to the things you want to see happen. *~Frank Lloyd Wright*

To succeed in your mission, you must have single-minded devotion to your goal. *~Abdul Kalam*

Quotes on Deceit

Those who makes promises they don't keep don't see the liar in the mirror. *~Robert McGinley*

They say is often a great liar. *~Proverb*

It is unfortunate, considering that enthusiasm moves the world, that so few enthusiasts can be trusted to speak the truth. *~Arthur Balfour*

Beware the fat man begging for food! *~Anonymous*

The greatest deception men suffer is from their own opinions. *~Leonardo DaVinci*

Quotes on Regret

Brotherly love is forgiveness without question until one's dead then the other questions himself. ~*Richard Briggs*

I'd rather regret the things I've done than regret the things I haven't done. ~*Lucille Ball*

Quotes on Failure

It's fine to celebrate success but it is more important to heed the lessons of failure. ~*Bill Gates*

Sometimes by losing a battle you find a new way to win the war. ~*Donald Trump*

It is impossible to live without failing at something, unless you live so cautiously that you might as well not have lived at all, in which case you have failed by default. ~*J.K. Rowling*

Quotes on Fear

If you know the enemy and know yourself you need not fear the results of a hundred battles. *~Sun Tzu*

Thinking will not overcome fear but action will. *~W Clement Stone*

Fear can be good when you're walking past an alley at night or when you need to check the locks on your doors before you go to bed, but it's not good when you have a goal and you're fearful of obstacles. We often get trapped by our fears, but anyone who has had success has failed before. *~Queen Latifah*

Quotes on Jealousy

I think it's important to get your surroundings as well as yourself into a positive state - meaning surround yourself with positive people, not the kind who are negative and jealous of everything you do. *~Heidi Klum*

The jealous are troublesome to others, but a torment to themselves. *~William Penn*

A competent and self-confident person is incapable of jealousy in anything. Jealousy is invariably a symptom of neurotic insecurity. *~Robert A Heinlein*

Jealousy is the fear of comparison. *~Max Frisch*

Jealousy is no more than feeling alone against smiling enemies. *~Elizabeth Bowen*

10 Quotes from Serial Killers

1. I sat down to think things over a bit. While I was sitting there, a little kid about eleven or twelve years-old came bumming around. He was looking for something. He found it too. I took him out to a gravel pit about one quarter miles away. I left him there, but first committed sodomy on him and then killed him. His brains were coming out of his ears when I left him, and he will never be any deader. ~*Carl Panzram*

Born June 28th 1891, Panzram was a convicted serial killer, arsonist, thief, burglar and rapist. Panzram confessed to his best friend and prison guard Henry Lesser to 22 murders and of sodomizing over 1000 young males. Of Prussian heritage, young Panzram was raised on a farm in Minnesota then was incarcerated several times for petty crimes. His killing spree began in 1920 when he started to lure young sailors from bars to rape and shoot them

2. Sometimes I feel like a vampire. ~*Ted Bundy*

Serial killer, rapist, kidnapper and necrophiliac, Theodore Robert Bundy confessed to 30 homicides across seven states during the early-'70s. Due to his handsome looks and charismatic behavior, the clinical psychopath found it easy to lure young women to his car. He often would have a fake plaster cast around his arm and would ask for the assistance of a young girl in helping him carry something to his car. Once there he would trap them inside his VW Beetle which he's modified by taking out the inside handles rendering the girls' escape futile. Blondie singer Debbie Harry had a fortunate escape from the killer unlike many of his victims who all resembled his former girlfriend, attractive, petite with mid-length brown hair in a center parting.

3. Sex is one of my downfalls. I get sex any way I can get it. If I have to force somebody to do it, I do…I rape them; I've done that.

I've killed animals to have sex with them, and I've had sex while they're alive. ~*Henry Lee Lucas*

Henry Lee Lucas was a murderer born in Blacksburg, Virginia. Born to alcoholic parents, including a mother who prostituted herself, Lucas's sexual deviancy formed in his teen years. In 1960, he was sentenced for the murder of his mother. Paroled in 1970, Lucas went back to jail for the attempted kidnapping of a 15-year-old girl. Released again in 1975, he killed two more women, and was arrested in 1983. He confessed to murdering hundreds of people, though no proof existed beyond three known victims. Lucas sat on Death Row, later changed to life in prison by Texas Governor George W. Bush. He died in a Texas prison from natural causes on March 12, 2001.

4. I just cut that woman from her neck down to her anus, I cut out her vagina, then I ate it. ~*Arthur Shawcross*

Arthur Shawcross' parents dispute his claims that he was molested as a child, but it's clear that he was troubled. In 1972, he confessed to killing two children and went to prison. His records were sealed so he could settle in a new town without causing a panic. But from 1988 to 1990, Shawcross killed 11 women in upstate New York, earning the nickname "The Genessee River Killer." He died in prison.

5. I remember there was actually a sexual thrill . . . you hear that little pop and pull their heads off and hold their heads up by the hair. Whipping their heads off, their body sitting there. That'd get me off. ~*Edmund Kemper*

Serial killer. Born Edmund Emil Kemper III in Burbank, California. During the 1970s, Edmund Kemper killed six young, college-age women in the Santa Cruz, California, area. In addition to the young women, he killed several members of his family and a family friend. Kemper committed his crimes in the same area and around the same time as two other serial killers, John Linley Frazier and Herbert Mullins. At the time, Santa

Cruz area became known as the "Murder Capital of the World" in the press and Kemper was dubbed the "Coed Killer" and the "Coed Butcher".

6. I would cook it, and look at the pictures and masturbate. *~Jeffrey Dahmer*

Jeffrey Lionel Dahmer, also known as the Milwaukee Cannibal, was an American serial killer and sex offender, who committed the rape, murder and dismemberment of seventeen men and boys between 1978 and 1991, with many of his later murders also involving necrophilia, cannibalism, and the permanent preservation of body parts—typically all or part of the skeletal structure. Dahmer was found to be legally sane at his trial. Convicted of fifteen of the sixteen murders he had committed in Wisconsin, Dahmer was sentenced to fifteen terms of life imprisonment on February 15, 1992. He was later sentenced to a sixteenth term of life imprisonment for an additional homicide committed in Ohio in 1978. On November 28, 1994, Dahmer was beaten to death in prison by Christopher Scarver, a fellow inmate at the Columbia Correctional Institution.

7. One day men will look back and say I gave birth to the twentieth century. *~Jack the Ripper*

From August 7 to September 10 in 1888, "Jack the Ripper" terrorized the Whitechapel district in London's East End. He killed at least five prostitutes and mutilated their bodies in an unusual manner, indicating that the killer had a knowledge of human anatomy. Jack the Ripper was never captured, and remains one of England's, and the world's, most infamous criminals. The culprit responsible for the murders of five prostitutes—all took place within a mile of each other, and involved the districts of Whitechapel, Spitalfields, Aldgate and the City of London—in London's East End in the autumn of 1888 he was never apprehended. Despite countless investigations claiming definitive evidence of the brutal killer's identity, his name and motive are still unknown. The moniker "Jack the Ripper" originates from a letter written by someone who claimed to be the

Whitechapel butcher, published at the time of the attacks. Adding to the mystery of the affair is the fact that several letters were sent by the killer to the London Metropolitan Police Service, also known as the Scotland Yard, taunting officers about his gruesome activities and speculating on murders to come. Various theories about Jack the Ripper's identity have been produced over the past several decades, which include claims accusing the famous Victorian painter Walter Sickert, a Polish migrant and even the grandson of Queen Victoria. Since 1888, more than 100 suspects have been named, contributing to widespread folklore and ghoulish entertainment surrounding the mystery.

8. The only thing they can get me for is running a funeral parlor without a license. *~JohnWayne Gacy*

John Wayne Gacy, known as "The Killer Clown", raped, tortured, and murdered at least 33 boys and men between 1972-78 in Chicago, IL. He was discovered by the police to have 29 bodies hidden in the crawl space of his house, and admitted to having killed more men which he disposed of in the river. He was executed by lethal injection in 1994.

9. I was born with the devil in me. I could not help the fact that I was a murderer, no more than a poet can help the inspiration to sing...I was born with the Evil One standing as my sponsor beside the bed where I was ushered into the world, and he has been with me since. *~H.H. Holmes*

Dr. H.H. Holmes confessed to 27 murders, and is believed to have killed as many as 200 people, during the time period surrounding the 1893 World's Fair in Chicago. Holmes ran a hotel equipped for killing- outfitted with gas lines into guest rooms, giant furnaces, lime and acid pits, and large vaults- and would torture, suffocate, and strangle his victims before disposing of them in the facility. Holmes was apprehended in Boston in 1894 and died by hanging in Philadelphia in 1896.

10. I love to kill people. I love to watch them die. I would shoot

them in the head and they would wiggle and squirm all over the place, and then just stop. Or I would cut them with a knife and watch their faces turn real white. I love all that blood. ~*Richard Ramirez*

Richard Ramirez, nicknamed the night stalker, went on a killing spree in the Los Angeles area that claimed the lives of at least 13 and as many as 16 in a spree that included shootings, mutilations, and rapes of his actual and intended victims. He was caught in East LA after his mugshot was broadcast across Southern California and he was accosted by a mob in the process of attempting to steal a car. He was tried, convicted, and died at 53 awaiting execution at San Quentin Prison.

Great Sports Quotes

Without self-discipline, success is impossible, period. ~*Lou Holtz*

Louis Holtz is a former college football coach and college football analyst for ESPN. He was the head coach at William and Mary college, NC State University, Arkansas University, Minnesota University, Notre Dame University, and the University of South Carolina. His college record is 249-132-7. Lou's University of Notre Dame 1988 team went 12-0 and was the national champion by consensus. He is the only college coach to lead 6 different programs to bowl games. Lou is also the only college coach to guide 4 different teams to the final top 20 rankings. Holtz is known for his ability to inspire players along with his quick wit.. Lou also coached the NY Jets in the 1976 season going 3-10 before going back to coaching college football. He was elected to the college football hall of fame in 2008.

During my 18 years I came to bat almost 10,000 times. I struck out about 1,700 times and walked maybe 1,800 times. You figure a ballplayer will average about 500 at bats a season. That means I played seven years without ever hitting the ball. ~*Mickey Mantle*

Mickey Mantle played professional baseball for the NY Yankees playing 1st base and center field for 17 years from 1951 through 1968. Mantle was one of the best players and sluggers, and is still regarded by many to be the greatest switch hitter in baseball history. Mickey was inducted into the baseball hall of fame in 1974 and was elected to the Major League Baseball All-Century Team in 1999. Mantle was noted for his ability to hit for both average and power. He hit 536 MLB career home runs, batted for over .300 or more ten times, and is tied with Jim Thome in walk-off home runs, with a combined thirteen, twelve in the regular season and one in the postseason. Mickey won the American League triple crown in 1956, leading the major leagues in batting average, home runs, and RBI's. He was an all star player for 16 seasons, playing in 16 of the 20 All-Star Games that were played. He won an American League gold glove in 1962 and was the

MVP of the American League three times. Mantle made 12 World Series appearances including 7 championships, and holds World Series records for the most home runs with 18, RBIs with 40, Runs with 42, extra base hits with 26, Walks with 43, and Total bases with 123. Mantle was the American League Home Run champion four times. He passed away at the age of 63.

Do you know what my favorite part of the game is? The opportunity to play. *~Mike Singletary*

Mike Singletary played football for Baylor University before being drafted and playing for the Chicago Bears in the NFL. He was the only junior to be selected to the all SouthWest Conference team of the 1970's. As a professional football player he was given the nickname "Samurai Mike" and the "Minister of Defense". He led the bears to a 15-1 season in 1985 where he recorded 109 solo tackles and 52 assists along with 3 sacks, 1 interception, a forced fumble, and 3 fumble recoveries. He won the defensive player of the year that year and again in 1988. He was elected to the college football hall of fame in 1998. He went on to be a linebackers coach for the Baltimore Ravens in 2003, in 2004 he became assistant coach of the San Francisco 49ers as well as their linebackers coach. In 2008 he became the interim head coach of the 49ers after then coach Mike Nolan was fired. He went on to post a 18-22 overall coaching record eventually being fired by the 49ers in 2010.

Just keep going. Everybody gets better if they keep at it. *~Ted Williams*

Theodore Samuel Williams played for the Boston Red Sox his entire career which spanned from 1939-1942 when he interrupted his career to serve in the marine corps and US Navy during WWII and resumed it when he returned in 1946 through 1960. He had many nicknames such as the "Greatest Hitter To Have Ever Lived" which to this day he is still held in such regard. Williams was a 17 time All Star, the American League MVP twice as well as the Triple Crown winner twice and the batting champion for 6 seasons. He hit for a career .344 average, hit 521 home runs, and his on base average of .482 is the highest of all time. He was inducted into the baseball hall of fame in 1966 and went on to manage the Washington Senators/Texas Rangers from 1969 to 1972. Williams passed away from a cardiac arrest in 2002 at the age of 83.

Don't quit. Suffer now and live the rest of your life as a champion.
~Muhammad Ali

Impossible is just a big word thrown around by small men who find it easier to live in the world they've been given than to explore the power they have to change it. Impossible is not a fact. It's an opinion. Impossible is not a declaration. It's a dare. Impossible is potential. Impossible is temporary. Impossible is nothing.
~Muhammad Ali

Muhammad Ali was born Cassius Marcellus Clay Jr in 1942. He began training at 12 years old and became the World Heavyweight Champion at age 22 beating Sonny Liston in an upset. Cassius joined the nation of Islam in 1973 and changed his name to Muhammad Ali. In 1967 Ali refused to be conscripted into the U.S. Military, citing his religious beliefs and his opposition to American involvement in the Vietnam war. The U.S. Judicial system failed to recognize him as a conscientious objector because Ali stated he would fight in a war if directed by Allah or Elijah Muhammad. He was arrested and found guilty of draft evasion and stripped of his Heavy Weight title. He didn't fight again for four years during his prime. In 1971 his appeal had made it to the Supreme Court where it was overturned and he returned to boxing. Ali's career boxing record is 56-5 with 37 KO's. Ali was an exceptional trash talker taunting opponents and baiting them before and during the match causing them to lose focus. Ali retired in 1979 and was diagnosed with Parkinson's disease in 1984, a disease that is common to head trauma. His health has severely declined over the years. He was recently hospitalized on January 15th of 2015 for a urinary tract infection after he was found unresponsive at a guest house in Scottsdale

AZ. He was released the next day.

Never let the fear of striking out get in your way. *~Babe Ruth*

Babe Ruth was born in 1942 in Baltimore MD. He played major league baseball for 22 years starting his career in the minors with the Baltimore Orioles in 1914 before being sold to the Boston Red Sox in 1916 where he gained notoriety as an outstanding pitcher who could occasionally hit home runs which was very uncommon in the 1920's era. He won 23 games twice in season with the Red Sox as well as winning 3 championships with the team as well but wanted to play ball on an everyday basis and was allowed to play the outfield. In 1919 he hit 29 home runs in 130 games, breaking the current record of 24 by Gavvy Cravath of the Phillies in 1915 and topping the total of 10 big league teams that year (Cravath had 12). Harry Frazee the owner of the Red Sox sold Ruth to the Yankees in the 1919-1920 offseason starting the "curse of the bambino" superstition that lasted until 2004 when the Red Sox came back from an 0-3 deficit to beat the Yankees in the American League Chamionship Series and go on to sweep the St. Louis Cardinals in the World Series ending a championship drought of 86 years. Babe finished his career with the Boston Braves. His career totals are 714 home runs, a career batting average of .342, 2,873 hits, 2,213 RBI's, a win-loss record of 94-46 with a n ERA of 2.28. He was a seven time World Series Champion, a 2 time all-star, The AL MVP in 1923 and the AL batting champion in 1924. He was the AL home run champion 12 times, The RBI champion 6 times, The ERA champion in 1916 and his number 3 jersey was retired by the NY Yankees. He is considered to be one the greatest baseball players of all time.

You're never a loser until you quit trying. *~Mike Ditka*

Mike Ditka was born Michael Keller Dyczko in 1939. His family changed the last name due to its difficult pronunciation. Mike played for the University of Pittsburgh from 1958 to1960 where he was a three sport athlete playing football, basketball, and baseball. He started all three seasons and led the team in receptions every year and also played at the punter position. He was drafted by the Chicago Bears fifth overall in the 1961 draft and went on to be the rookie of the year. He was selected to the pro bowl 5 times. He also played for the Philadelphia Eagles and the Dallas Cowboys. He won a championship with the 1963 Bears and a Super Bowl Chamionship with the Dallas Cowboys in Super Bowl VI where he scored a touchdown. To this day he is still the only head coach to have ever scored a Super Bowl touchdown. He retired playing after the 1972 season and was hired as an assistant head coach under Tom Landry with the Cowboys where he spent 9 seasons and in 8 of them they made the playoffs with 6 division titles, 3 NFC championships and a Super Bowl Championship in 1977. He was hired as the head coach of the Chicago Bears in 1982 and won the Super Bowl 4 years later defeating the New England Patriots 46-10 in Super Bowl XX. His career record as a head coach of the bears was 106-62 making the playoffs 7 out of the 11 years he coached there. The bears retired his jersey in 2013 which will be the last Chicago Bears jersey number to ever be retired.

To me, there are three things we all should do every day. We should do this every day of our lives. Number one is laugh. You should laugh every day. Number two is think. You should spend some time in thought. And number three is, you should have your emotions moved to tears, could be happiness or joy. But think about it. If you laugh, you think, and you cry, that's a full day. That's a heck of a day. You do that seven days a week, you're going to have something special ~*Jim Valvano*

Jim Valvano was a college basketball player, coach, and broadcaster. He played for Rutgers University as a point guard, after graduating he started his coaching career at Johns Hopkins University in Baltimore for 1 season. The next 2 years he was an assistant coach at Conneticut, from there he went on to head coach the Bucknell, Iona, and eventually NC State Programs. "Coach V" as he was known was voted the ACC coach of the ear in 1989. His overall coaching win-loss record was 346-210. He retired from coaching in 1990 and went into broadcasting working for ABC Sports and ESPN. In 1992 he won a Cable Ace Award for commentator/analyst for his NCAA broadcasts. Jim was diagnosed with cancer in June of 1992 (adenocarcinoma).

On March 3rd 1993 he gave his legendary inaugural ESPY speech while accepting the Arthur Ashe Courage and Humanitarian Award which the quote above was a part of along with his closing quote "Cancer can take away all of my physical abilities. It cannot touch my mind, it cannot touch my heart, and it cannot touch my soul. And those three things are going to carry on forever. I thank you and God bless you all." The crowd gave him a standing ovation. He died April 28th 1993 at Duke University in Raleigh North Carolina.

A good hockey player plays where the puck is. A great hockey player plays where the puck is going to be. *~Wayne Gretzky*

Procrastination is one of the most common and deadliest of diseases and its toll on success and happiness is heavy. *~Wayne Gretzky*

Wayne Gretzky was born in 1961, he played in the National Hockey League from 1979-1999. He started his career with the Edmonton Oilers where he revolutionized the game of hockey into a team strategy based style of play. The style of play in the NHL had been focused on the player with the puck. Gretzky wasn't the biggest, strongest, or fastest by any means of a lot of other players in the era. Gretzky took the focus off of himself by passing the puck to his teammates where once he had passed the puck to a teammate he would dart to an open area of ice effectively negating his lack of size, strength, and speed. The Edmonton Oilers went on to average 423 goals per season from 1982 to 1985 when no team had previously ever scored 400. Gretzky during that time averaged 207 points a year when no player had ever eclipsed the 152 point mark. Gretzky amassed 894 goals and 1,963 assists for a total of 2,857 points in his career, to put that in perspective the number 2 all time scorer is Mark Messier with 1,887 points who played in 269 more games, *almost 1,000 points behind Gretzky's points totals plus a special mention that Gretzky's assists totals are more than any other players career points totals. Gretzky scored 92 goals in a season, the most ever scored in a single season by a player. Gretzky scored 163 assists in a single season, 2nd is Mario Lemieux with a 114 assists in a single season. Gretzky actually has 10 out of the top 11 all time single season assist records before tying Bobby Orr with 102 assists for 12th all time most assists in a single season. He holds the top 4 most points in a season records scoring 215, 212, 208, and 205 points in a season. Mario Lemieux is 5th on the all-time most points scored in a single season list with 199 points. Gretzky holds 9 out of the top 11 in this category, Mario Lemieux holds the 5th and 8th spots. Wayne was traded to the L.A. Kings in 1988 where he won one of his four Stanley Cup championships, the other three were with Edmonton. The trade brought an influx of fans in the California market where shortly thereafter the San Jose Sharks and Anaheim Ducks were added to the league. Gretzky currently holds 61 NHL records almost all of which are considered unbreakable. Gretzky's number 99 jersey was retired by the NHL upon his retirement, he is the only NHL player to have that honor. Also upon retirement he bypassed the three year waiting list and was inducted into the hockey hall of fame. The NHL announced that he will be the last player that it will be done for. Wayne's primary residence is in Southern California though he does also own homes in Arizona and Missouri.*

Gold medals aren't really made of gold. They're made of sweat, determination, and a hard-to-find alloy called guts. ~*Dan Gable*

Dan Gable won the Olympic Gold medal in the 1972 Olympic games held in Munich, Germany where he didn't give up a single point. Dan's wrestling career started as a high school freshman where he wasn't allowed to play on the varsity squad. His freshman year he had his only recorded loss of his high school career to then state champion Matt Leamon. In his sophomore year tragedy hit when his sister Diane was molested and murdered by one of Dan's classmates, John Thomas Kyle in their home while Dan and the family were on vacation. Dan later recalled that the event gave him a singular passion for wrestling as a way to uplift his shattered family. Over the next three years of high school he went 64-0. His sophomore year he won individual class AA state champion 95 lbs. His junior year he did the same but at 103 lbs. and his senior year he did it again at 112 lbs. In his junior and senior years they were team state champions. Dan went on to wrestle at Iowa State University. He again was not permitted to play varsity his freshman year. He posted a 181-1 record at Iowa State losing only his final collegiate match to Washington University's Larry Owings. Iowa State won 2 NCAA titles during his three varsity years. Dan went on to wrestle in the national freestyle circuit from 1967 to 1976 with a 67-4 record. In 1971 to 1973 Dan wrestled on the international circuit posting a 30-1 record. Overall his freestyle record was 97-5. Before his Olympic gold medal in 1972 the Soviet Union had promised to scour the entire Eastern bloc to find a wrestler to take down Dan Gable. They were unsuccessful in doing so and were also unable to score a point on Dan though nor did anyone else. Russia's Ruslan Ashuraliyev won the bronze with Japan's Kikuo Wada taking silver. In 1976 Dan became Iowa State University's wrestling coach and would become the greatest coach in collegiate history, from 1978 to 1986 Iowa State University won the NCAA title 9 straight years in a row. He coached until 1993 when he took a sabbatical due to injuries that kept him from coaching with a hands on approach that he thought his teams deserved. His teams compiled a dual meet record of 355–21–5. He coached 152 all-Americans, 45 national champions, 106 Big Ten Champions and 12 Olympians, including four gold, one silver and three bronze medalists.

You can't put a limit on anything. The more you dream, the farther you get. ~*Michael Phelps*

Michael Phelps is the most decorated Olympian athlete of all time with 22 medals. Phelps holds the all time record for gold medals with 18, double that of the next closest competitor. Michael won 8 gold medals at the 2008 Beijing Olympics, the most first place finishes for any olympic athlete at any olympic games. Currently, he holds seven world records, not including his records for most Olympic medals and most Olympic gold medals ever won by one person. Three of those seven world records are in individual events; The 100 and 200 meter butterfly with times of 49.82 seconds and 1:51.51 seconds respectively and the individual medley with a time of 4:03.84 seconds.

I am building a fire, and everyday I train, I add more fuel. At just the right moment, I light the match. *~Mia Hamm*

Mia Hamm was named the women's player of the year the first two years the award was given out in 2001 and 2002. She is second in most international goals (men or women) behind Abby Wambach who broke Mia's record in 2013 scoring her 159th goal. Mia was also given the FIFA world player of the year the first two years that award was give also in 2001 and 2002. She has been inducted into the National Soccer Hall Of Fame, the Texas Sports Hall Of Fame, and the World Football Hall Of Fame, she was the first woman ever inducted into the World Football Hall Of Fame. She was one of only two females named to the FIFA 100, a list of the greatest 125 living soccer players as named by Pele.

One man practicing sportsmanship is far better than a hundred teaching it. *~Knute Rockne*

Knute Rockne was born in Voss, Norway and his family emigrated to the United States when he was five. He lived in the Logan's Square area of Chicago, learning to play football in his neighborhood. He played football in high school as well as track. He attended Notre Dame college where he excelled playing the end position gaining All-American honors in 2013. He also helped to transform the collegiate game at the time which was a heavy running game with scarce use of the passing play in a single game where Notre Dame quarterback Charlie "Gus" Dorais hooked up with Rockne time and time again to stun the

highly regarded Army team 35-13. Knute graduated Notre Dame with a degree in Pharmacy. He worked as a lab assistant at Notre Dame taking the football coaching job when it was offered to him. During thirteen years as head coach he went 102-12-5 also winning three national championships as well as five undefeated seasons without a tie. He posted the highest winning percentage at .881 for an American FBS/Division I college football coach. He made his coaching debut on September 28, 1918, against Case Tech in Cleveland earning a 26-6 victory. In the backfield was Leonard Bahan, George Gipp, and Curly Lambeau. The 1919 team went undefeated and were a national champion. Gipp died December 14, 1920, just two weeks after being elected Notre Dame's first All-American by Walter Camp. Gipp contracted strep throat and pneumonia. Since antibiotics were not available in the 1920s, treatment options for such infections were limited and they could be fatal even to young, healthy individuals. It was while on his hospital bed and speaking to Rockne that he is purported to have delivered the famous,"win just one for the Gipper" line. On November 10, 1928, when the "Fighting Irish" team was losing to Army 6-0 at the end of the half, Rockne entered the locker room and told the team the words he heard on Gipp's deathbed in 1920: "I've got to go, Rock. It's all right. I'm not afraid. Some time, Rock, when the team is up against it, when things are going wrong and the breaks are beating the boys, tell them to go in there with all they've got and win just one for the Gipper. I don't know where I'll be then, Rock. But I'll know about it, and I'll be happy." This inspired the team, which then outscored Army in the second half and won the game 12-6. The phrase "Win one for the Gipper" was later used as a political slogan by Ronald Reagan, who in 1940 portrayed Gipp in Knute Rockne, All American.

If you are afraid of failure you don't deserve to be successful!
~Charles Barkley

Charles Wade Barkley established himself as one of the NBA's most dominating power forwards. He's been selected to the All-NBA All Star team five times, The All-NBA second team five times, and the All-NBA third team once playing in eleven All Star games. He was the All Star MVP in 1991. In 1993 he was voted the leagues most valuable player. He was voted one of the fifty greatest NBA players in its 50 year history. He played in the 1992 and 1996 Olympics capturing gold medals in both as part of the "Dream team". He is one of only five players to amass 20,000 points, 10,000 rebounds, and 4,000 assists.

Today I will do what others won't, so tomorrow I can accomplish what others can't. ~*Jerry Rice*

Jerry Rice is considered one of the greatest wide receivers to have ever played the game. In 2010 NFL networks NFL films named him as the greatest wide receiver and among one of the greatest NFL players in NFL history. He was selected to the Pro Bowl thirteen times, twelve times All Pro in his twenty year career. He won three Super Bowl rings with the San Francisco 49ers and an AFC championship with the Oakland Raiders. Rice holds over 100 NFL records, the most of any player by a wide margin.

Talent is God given. Be humble. Fame is man-given. Be grateful. Conceit is self-given. Be careful. ~*John Wooden*

John Wooden played collegiate basketball at Purdue University where he was a three time consensus All American. He also coached UCLA where he was nicknamed the Wizard of Westwood. He won ten National championships during a twelve year period including seven in a row. This is quite an accomplishment as no team or coach have won more than two in a row. His team won an astounding 88 consecutive games during his tenure. He was named National Coach of the Year six times. He was the first person to ever be named into the Basketball Hall of Fame as a coach and as a player. He is one of the most revered coaches in the history of sports, beloved by his former players for his simple teachings directed for hi players to be successful in life as well as basketball. In 2009, Wooden was named The Sporting News's Greatest Coach of All Time.

There may be people that have more talent than you, but there's no excuse for anyone to work harder than you do. *~Derek Jeter*

Derek Sanderson Jeter is a former professional baseball shortstop who played 20 seasons in Major League Baseball for the New York Yankees. A five-time World Series champion, Jeter is regarded as a central figure of the Yankees' success of the late 1990s and early 2000's for his hitting, baserunning, fielding, and leadership. He's the Yankees' all-time career leader in hits with 3,465, doubles with 544, games played 2,747, stolen bases 358, times on base 4,716, plate appearances 12,602 and at bats 11,195. He's a fourteen time All-Star, with five Gold Glove Awards, five Silver Slugger Awards, two Hank Aaron Awards, and a Roberto Clemente Award. He became the 28th player to reach 3,000 hits and finished his career sixth all-time in career hits and the all-time MLB leader in hits by a shortstop. In 1996 he won the Rookie of the Year award. In 2000 he won the All Star Game MVP award as well as the MVP for the World Series.

If you train hard, you'll not only be hard, you'll be hard to beat. *~Herschel Walker*

Herschel Walker won the Heisman Trophy in 1982 at the University of Georgia. He played professional football first with the New Jersey Generals of the USFL before going into the NFL where he played for the Minnesota Vikings, Philadelphia Eagles, Dallas Cowboys, and New York Giants. He was inducted into the College Football Hall of Fame in 1999. He later went on to fight two MMA fights and went 2-0 both wins coming via TKO.

I've got a theory that if you give 100% all of the time, somehow things will work out in the end. *~Larry Bird*

Larry Joe Bird played in the NBA for the Boston Celtics his entire career playing small and power forward. He was a twelve time NBA All Star and named the league's MVP three consecutive years from 1984 through 1986. He won three championships and two NBA Finals MVP's. He won a gold medal as part of the 1992 US Mens Olympic Basketball team also known as the Dream Team. He was voted to the NBA's 50th Anniversary All-Time Team in 1996. He was the Indian Pacers head coach from 1997 to 2000. He became the president of basketball operations for the Pacers in 2003 through 2012 when he retired. He is the only person in NBA history to be named Most Valuable Player, Coach of the Year, and Executive of the Year.

Whoever said, 'It's not whether you win or lose that counts, probably lost. ~*Martina Navratilova*

Martina Navratilova is a retired Czech and American tennis player and coach. In 2005, Tennis magazine selected her as the greatest female tennis player for the years 1965 through 2005. Navratilova was ranked World No. 1 for a total of 332 weeks in singles, and a record 237 weeks in doubles, making her the only player in history to have held the top spot in both singles and doubles for over 200 weeks. She was year-end singles No. 1 seven times, including a record five consecutive years, as well as year-end doubles No. 1 five times, including three consecutive years during which she held the ranking for the entire year. She won 18 Grand Slam singles titles, 31 major women's doubles titles which is an an all-time record, and 10 major mixed doubles titles. She reached the Wimbledon singles final twelve times, including nine consecutive years from 1982 through 1990, and won the women's singles title at Wimbledon a record nine times including a run of six consecutive titles – the best performance by any professional player at a major event. Her and Billie Jean King each won 20 Wimbledon titles, an all-time record. Navratilova is one of just three women ever to have accomplished a Career Grand Slam in singles, women's doubles, and mixed doubles, a distinction she shares with Margaret Court and Doris Hart. Navratilova holds the records for most singles titles with 167 and for most doubles titles with 177 in the open era. Her record as number one in singles from 1982 to 1986 is the most dominant in professional tennis. Over five consecutive seasons, she won 428 of 442 singles matches, averaging fewer than three losses per year to 87 wins, for a sustained winning percentage of 96.8%. She holds the best season win-loss record for the open era, 86-1, a 98.9% winning percentage in 1983, and four of the top six open era seasons. She recorded the longest winning streak in the open era winning 74 consecutive matches and three of the six longest winning streaks. She is the only professional player to have won six major singles crowns without the loss of a set. Navratilova, Margaret Court and Maureen Connolly share the record for the most consecutive major singles titles with six. Navratilova reached 11 consecutive major singles finals, second all-time to Steffi Graf's 13, and is the only woman ever to reach 19 consecutive major semi-finals. Navratilova also won the season-ending World Tennis Association Tour Championships for top ranked players a record eight times and made the finals a record fourteen times. She is the only person of either sex to have won eight different tournaments at least seven times. She was ranked in the world's top ten in singles for a record twenty consecutive years from 1975 to 1994, a span which included 19 years in the top five, 15 years in the top three, and 7 years as the world No.1 ranked singles player. In women's doubles, Navratilova and Pam Shriver won 109 consecutive matches and won all four major titles—the Grand Slam in 1984. The pair set an all-time record of 79 titles together and tied Louise Brough Clapp's and Margaret Osborne duPont's record of 20 major women's doubles titles as a team. Navratilova also won the WTA Tour Championships doubles title a record eleven times. She is one of only five tennis players all-time to win a multiple slam set in two disciplines, matching Margaret Court, Roy Emerson, Frank Sedgman and Serena Williams. Navratilova took her last major title in 2006, winning the mixed doubles crown at the 2006 US Open, just short of her 50th birthday, 32 years after her first Grand Slam title in 1974.

To succeed...You need to find something to hold on to, something to motivate you, something to inspire you. ~*Tony Dorsett*

Tony Dorsett was drafted second overall by the Dallas Cowboys in the 1977 draft after a successful high school and college career at Hopewell High School and the University of Pittsburgh. He played basketball and football in high school. When he became a sophomore the coaches believed him to be too small to play running back and moved him to cornerback. In 1971 he won the running back position when he took a screen pass 75 yards for a touchdown in the season opener. Tony continued to play cornerback as well. He rushed for 1.034 yards and 19 touchdowns that year and was named All State. He also led his basketball team to the WPIAL quarterfinals that year. In 1972 he again was selected All State. He set a single game rushing record with 247 yards and a single season rushing record with 1,238 yards. He was also a key defensive player as a linebacker. Hopewell High School retired his number 33 jersey and renamed their stadium after him. At Pitt University he was named All-American, the first time a freshman had done so in 29 years. He finished second in rushing with 1,586 yards and helped lead the team to its first winning season in ten years. His 1,586 yards were the most ever recorded by a freshman. As a senior he helped lead his school to a national title in 1976, picking up the Heisman Trophy, the Maxwell Award, the Walter Camp Award for Player of the Year, and the United Press International Player of the Year award along the way as he led the nation in rushing with 2,150 yards. He was a three-time first-team All-American in 1973, 1975, and 1976 and a second-team All-American in 1974 by UPI and Newspaper Enterprise Association. Dorsett finished his college career with 6,082 total rushing yards, then an NCAA record. This would stand as the record until it was surpassed by Ricky Williams in 1998. Dorsett is considered one of the greatest running backs in college football history. In 2007, he was ranked #7 on ESPN's Top 25 Players in College Football History list. In 1994, he was inducted into the College Football Hall of Fame. In his rookie season with the Dallas Cowboys he rushed for a 1,007 yards and scored 12 touchdowns and won rookie of the year. He was the first person to win the college football championship one year and the Super Bowl the next. His second year with the Cowboys he rushed for 1,325 yards and scored seven touchdowns. In 1981 he rushed for 1,646 yards breaking the Cowboys franchise record, it was his most productive season in his career. Dorsett ended his career with 12, 739 yards and 77 touchdowns. He made the Pro Bowl four times in his career and was inducted into the NFL hall of fame in 1994.

My mind is my biggest asset. I expect to win every tournament I play. *~Tiger Woods*

Eldrick Tont "Tiger" Woods is an American professional golfer who is among the most successful golfers of all time. Following an outstanding amateur and two-year college golf career, Woods turned professional at age 20 in late summer of 1996. By April 1997 he had already won his first major, the 1997 Masters in a record-breaking performance, winning the tournament by 12 strokes. He first reached the number one position in the world rankings in June 1997. Through the 2000s, Woods was the dominant force in golf, spending 264 weeks from August 1999 to September 2004 and 281 weeks from June 2005 to October 2010 as world number one. From December 2009 to early April 2010, Woods took leave from professional golf to focus on his marriage after he admitted infidelity, but he and his wife Elin Nordegren eventually divorced. This was followed by a loss of golf form, and his ranking gradually fell to a low of No. 58 in November 2011. He ended a career-high winless streak of 107 weeks when he captured the Chevron World Challenge in December 2011. After winning the Arnold Palmer Invitational on March 25, 2013, he ascended to the No.1 ranking once again, holding the top spot until May 2014. Woods had back disc surgery in April 2014, and has struggled since to regain his dominant form. By March 29, 2015, Woods had fallen to #104, outside of the top 100 for the first time since the week prior to his first Tour title win in 1996. Woods has broken numerous golf records. He has been World Number One for the most consecutive weeks and for the greatest total number of weeks of any golfer. He has been awarded PGA Player of the Year a record eleven times, the Byron Nelson Award for lowest adjusted scoring average a record eight times, and has the record of leading the money list in ten different seasons. He has won 14 professional major golf championships, the second highest of any player behind Jack Nicklaus with 18, and 79 PGA

Tour events, second all time behind Sam Snead's 82 wins. He has more career major wins and career PGA Tour wins than any other active golfer. He is the youngest player to achieve the career Grand Slam, and the youngest and fastest to win 50 tournaments on tour. Additionally, Woods is only the second golfer, after Jack Nicklaus, to have achieved a career Grand Slam three times. Woods has won 18 World Golf Championships, and won at least one of those events in each of the first 11 years after they began in 1999. Woods and Rory McIlroy are the only golfers to win both The Silver Medal and The Gold Medal at The Open Championship.

I've always believed that if you put in the work, the results will come. *~Michael Jordan*

Never say never, because limits, like fears, are often just illusion. *~Michael Jordan*

Michael Jeffrey Jordan played fifteen seasons in the NBA and is now the principal owner of the Charlotte Hornets. In 1991 he won his first championship with the Chicago Bulls then again in 1992 and 1993 for his first of two three-peats. He went to Elmsley A. Laney High School where he played basketball, baseball, and football. As a sophomore he didn't make the varsity basketball team as he was deemed to short at that time to play at that level, he was 5'11". Motivated to prove his worth he became the star of the junior varsity team posting several 40 point performances. That summer he sprouted four inches while training rigorously. His junior year he earned a varsity spot and averaged twenty points per game over the next two years. His senior year he averaged a triple double in points with 29.2 per game, rebounds with 11.6 per game, and assists with 10.1 per game and was selected to the McDonald's All American Team. He was recruited by numerous colleges accepting a scholarship to North Carolina. He was named Freshman of the year his first season and made the championship game winning shot in the 1982 NCAA tournament. This moment he later described as the major turning point in his basketball career. During his three seasons at NC he averaged 17.7 points and 5 rebounds per game while shooting 54%. His sophomore and junior seasons he was selected to the All-American First Team by consensus. In 1984 Jordan left NC one year early to enter the 1984 NBA draft. He was selected third overall behind Hakeem Olajuwon drafted by the Houston Rockets and Sam Bowie drafted by the Portland Trailblazers due to the fact that the Rockets and Trailblazers were both in need of centers. In Jordan's first season with the bulls he averaged 28.2 points and the Bulls were swept by the Milwaukee Bucks 4-0 in the first round of the playoffs. In his second season he broke his foot early in the season and missed 64 games. That year in the playoffs they were swept by the legendary 1985-1986 Boston Celtics even with Jordan scoring a still unbroken record high 63 points in game 2. After fully recovering from his foot injury he had a monster season in his third year becoming one of only two players in NBA history to score 3,000 points in a season, the other being Wilt Chamberlain. Jordan averaged a league high 37.1 points per game and also displayed his defensive prowess becoming the first player in NBA history to record 200 steals and 100 blocks in a season. Despite these numbers Magic Johnson won the league's MVP that year. This year's playoffs they would again be swept by the Celtics. Jordan led the league again in scoring the following year averaging 35 points per game this time winning MVP and Defensive Player of the Year averaging 1.6 blocks per game and a league high 3.16 steals per game. This year they made it out of the first round of the playoffs defeating the Cleveland Cavaliers in 5 games before losing to the Detroit Pistons in 5. In the following season of 1988-1989 he led the league in scoring again averaging 32.5 points per game along with 8 rebounds and assists per game. This year they made it to the Eastern Conference Finals again losing to the Detroit Pistons this time in 6 games. In the 1989-1990 season Jordan averaged a league high 33.6 points per game as well as 6.9 rebounds per game and 6.3 assists per game. Chicago again made it to the Eastern Conference Finals again losing to Detroit this time in 7 games. In the 1990-1991 season, Jordan won his second MVP award after averaging 31.5 ppg, 6.0 rpg, and 5.5 apg for the regular season. The Bulls finished in first place in their division for the first time in 16 years and set a franchise record with 61 wins in the regular season. With Scottie Pippen developing into an All-Star, the Bulls had elevated their play. The Bulls defeated the New York Knicks and the Philadelphia 76ers in the opening two rounds of the playoffs. They advanced to the Eastern Conference Finals where their rival, the Detroit Pistons, awaited them. However, this time the Bulls beat the Pistons in a four-game sweep. The Bulls advanced to the NBA Finals for the first time in franchise history to face Magic Johnson and James Worthy and beat the Los Angeles Lakers four games to one, compiling an outstanding 15–2 playoff record along the way. Perhaps the best known moment of the series came in Game 2 when, attempting a dunk, Jordan avoided a potential Sam Perkins block by switching the ball from his right hand to his left in mid-air to lay the shot in. In his first Finals appearance, Jordan posted per game averages of 31.2 points, 11.4 assists, 6.6 rebounds, 2.8 steals and 1.4 blocks. Jordan won his first NBA Finals MVP award. Jordan and the Bulls continued their dominance in the 1991–92 season, establishing a 67–15 record, topping their franchise record from 1990 to 91. Jordan won his second consecutive MVP award with averages of 30.1 points, 6.4 rebounds and 6.1 assists per game on 52% shooting. After winning a physical 7-game series over the New York Knicks in the second round of the playoffs and finishing off the Cleveland Cavaliers in the Conference Finals in 6 games, the Bulls met Clyde Drexler and the Portland Trail Blazers in the Finals. The media, hoping to recreate a Magic–Bird rivalry, highlighted the similarities between "Air" Jordan and Clyde "The Glide" during the pre-Finals hype. In the first game, Jordan scored a Finals-record 35 points in the first half, including a record-setting six three-point field goals. The Bulls went on to win Game 1, and defeat the Blazers in six games. Jordan was named Finals MVP for the second year in a row and finished the series averaging 35.8 ppg, 4.8 rpg, and 6.5 apg. In the 1992–93 season, despite a 32.6 ppg, 6.7 rpg and 5.5 apg campaign, Jordan's streak of consecutive MVP seasons ended as he lost the award to his friend Charles Barkley. Coincidentally, Jordan and the Bulls met Barkley and his Phoenix Suns in the 1993 NBA Finals. The Bulls *won their third NBA championship on a game-winning shot by John Paxson and a last-second block by Horace Grant, but Jordan was once again Chicago's leader. He averaged a Finals-record 41.0 ppg during the six-game series, and became the first player in NBA history to win three straight Finals MVP awards. He scored more than 30 points in every game of the series, including 40 or more points in 4 consecutive games. With his third Finals triumph, Jordan capped off a seven-year run where he attained seven scoring titles and three championships, but there were signs that Jordan was tiring of his massive celebrity and all of the non-basketball hassles in his life. On October 6th 1993 Jordan announced his retirement. He cited he lost his desire to play the game. He signed a minor league contract with the Chicago White Sox in 1994 and reported to their spring training in Sarasota, Fl. He was assigned to the team's minor league team. He finished with a .202 batting average with 3 home runs, 51 RBI's, 30 stolen bases, and 11 errors. In November of 1994 his number 23 was retired by the Chicago Bulls. In March of 1995 Jordan quit baseball and returned to the NBA now wearing number 45 as his number 23 had been retired. He helped his team late in the season winning 13 of the last 17 games to make it into the playoffs. They advanced to the Eastern Conference Championship and were beaten by the Orlando Magic in 6 games. Jordan trained hard in the off-season motivated by the playoff loss and the Bulls next season they set an NBA all time record going 72-10. Jordan again led the league in scoring averaging 30.4 ppg winning the MVP and the All Star MVP. The Bulls lost only 3 games in 4 series in the playoffs and won the championship with Jordan being named the finals MVP a record setting 4th time. In the 1996-1997 season the Bulls went 69-13 and Jordan was beat out for league MVP by Karl Malone. They again won the championship and Jordan was again named the Finals MVP for the 5th time in 5 finals appearances. In that years All Star game Jordan scored the first ever triple double in an All Star game in NBA history however he didn't win the MVP award. In the 1997-1998 season the Bulls went 62-20 with Jordan leading the league in scoring again with 28.7 ppg* *winning his 5th regular season MVP award. That year in the playoffs they went to a game 7 against Reggie Miller's Pacers in the Eastern Conference Finals. His first game 7 series since the Knicks in1992. They went on to face the Utah Jazz in the Finals with Jordan hitting a jump shot over a couple Jazz defenders cutting Utah's lead to 86-85. The Jazz then went downcourt and passed the ball to Karl Malone who was being defended by Dennis Rodman. Rodman and Malone tussled as Malone caught the pass, Jordan cut behind Malone*

and stole the ball dribbling down court and stopping at the top of the key before hitting the game winning shot with 5.2 seconds left on the clock. The Jazz missed a desperation three point attempt and The Bulls completed a second three-peat with Jordan again being named the Finals MVP. In 1999 Jordan retired a second time. In 2000 he returned to the NBA as part owner and president of basketball operations for the Washington Wizards. In 2001 he returned to the court but was injury plagued and played in 60 games starting in 53 of them. He averaged 24.3 ppg, 5.4 apg, and 6 rpg. He finished his playing career in the 2002-2003 season. In his last game at First Union Center against the Philadelphia 76ers the crowd starting chanting "we want Mike" just after the start of the 4th quarter as he was on the bench after scoring 13 points in the game. With 2:35 remaining in the game Jordan reentered the game and was intentionally fouled by the 76ers Eric Snow. Jordan went to the free throw line and sunk both shots. Right after the second free throw shot the ball was inbounded and the player intentionally fouled to let Jordan return to the bench. Jordan received a three-minute standing ovation from his teammates, his opponents, the officials and the crowd of 21,257 fans.

Everybody pulls for David, nobody roots for Goliath. *~Wilt Chamberlain*

Wilton Norman Chamberlain was an American basketball player. He played for the University of Kansas and also for the Harlem Globetrotters before playing in the NBA. In the NBA he played

for the Philadelphia/San Francisco Warriors, the Philadelphia 76ers, and the Los Angeles Lakers. The 7 foot 1 inch Chamberlain weighed 250 pounds as a rookie before bulking up to 275 and eventually to over 300 pounds with the Lakers. He played the center position and is widely considered one of the greatest and most dominant players in NBA history. Chamberlain holds numerous NBA records in scoring, rebounding and durability categories. He is the only player to score 100 points in a single NBA game or average more than 40 and 50 points in a season. He also won seven scoring, nine field goal percentage, and eleven rebounding titles, and led the league in assists once. Chamberlain is the only player in NBA history to average at least 30 points and 20 rebounds per game in a season, a feat he accomplished seven times. He is also the only player to average at least 30 points and 20 rebounds per game over the entire course of his NBA career. He won two championships, four regular season MVP awards, the Rookie of the year award, and a Finals MVP award along with being selected to the All Star team 13 times.

The pitcher has got only a ball. I've got a bat. So the percentage of weapons is in my favor and I let the fellow with the ball do the fretting. *~Hank Aaron*

Henry Louis Aaron is a retired American Major League Baseball right fielder. He played 21 seasons for the Milwaukee/Atlanta Braves in the National League and 2 seasons for the Milwaukee Brewers in the American League (AL), from 1954 through 1976. Aaron held the MLB record for career home runs for 33 years, and he still holds several MLB offensive records. He hit 24 or more home runs every year from 1955 through 1973, and is one of only two players to hit 30 or more home runs in a season at least fifteen times. In 1999, The Sporting News ranked Aaron fifth on its 100 Greatest Baseball Players list. Aaron was an NL All-Star for 20 seasons and an AL All-Star for 1 season, from 1955 through 1975. Aaron holds the record for the most seasons as an All-Star WITH 21, the most All-Star Game selections with 25, and is tied with Willie Mays and Stan Musial for the most All-Star Games played with 24. He was a Gold Glove winner for three seasons. In 1957, he was the NL Most Valuable Player when the Milwaukee Braves won the World Series. He won the NL Player of the Month award in May 1958 and June 1967. Aaron holds the MLB records for the most career runs batted in with 2,297, extra base hits with 1,477, and total bases with 6,856. Aaron is also in the top five for career hits with 3,771 and runs with 2,174. He is one of only four players to have at least seventeen seasons with 150 or more hits. Aaron is in second place in home runs at 755 and at-bats with 12,364, and in third place in games playing 3,298 games. At the time of his retirement, Aaron held most of the game's key career power hitting records. Since his retirement, Aaron has held front office roles with the Atlanta Braves. He was inducted into the National Baseball Hall of Fame in 1982. In 1999, MLB introduced the Hank Aaron Award to recognize the top offensive players in each league. He was awarded the Presidential Medal of Freedom in 2002. He was named a 2010 Georgia Trustee by the Georgia Historical Society in recognition of accomplishments that reflect the ideals of Georgia's founders.

What makes a good coach? Complete dedication. *~George Halas*

George Halas was a player, coach, owner, and a pioneer in professional American Football. He was the iconic founder and owner of the National Football League's Chicago Bears. He was also lesser known as an inventor, jurist, producer, philanthropist, philatelist, and Major League Baseball player. Most notably, he is considered one of the original co-founders of the National Football League in 1922.

In both 1963 and 1965 he was selected by The Sporting News, the AP and the UPI as the NFL Coach of the Year. In 1997 he was featured on a U.S. postage stamp as one of the legendary coaches of football. He has been recognized by ESPN as one of the ten most influential people in sports in the 20th century, and as one of the greatest coaches. In 1993, Miami Dolphins coach Don Shula finally surpassed Halas' victory total. To this day, the jerseys of the Chicago Bears bear the initials "GSH" on their upper left sleeves in commemoration of Halas.

I have nothing in common with lazy people who blame others for their lack of success. Great things come from hard work and perseverance. No excuses. ~*Kobe Bryant*

Kobe Bryant is a professional basketball player for the Los Angeles Lakers of the National Basketball Association. He entered the NBA directly from high school, and he has played for the Lakers his entire career, winning five NBA championships. Bryant is a 17-time All-Star, 15-time member of the All-NBA Team, and 12-time member of the All-Defensive team. He has led the league in scoring twice, and he ranks third on both the league's all-time regular season scoring and all-time postseason scoring lists. Bryant set an NBA record for the most seasons with one team in his 20th season the same season he announced he would retire. At 34 years and 104 days, Bryant became the youngest player in league history to reach 30,000 career points. He's also the all time leading scorer in Lakers franchise history. Since his second year in the league, Bryant has been selected to start every All Star Game. He has won the All Star MVP Award four times in 2002, 2007, 2009, and 2011, tying him for the most All Star MVP Awards in NBA history. At the 2008 and 2012 Summer Olympics, he won gold medals as a member of the U.S. national team. Sporting News and TNT named Bryant the top NBA player of the 2000s.

If you don't invest very much, then defeat doesn't hurt very much and winning is not very exciting. ~*Dick Vermeil*

Richard Albert "Dick" Vermeil is a retired American head coach for the National Football League's Philadelphia Eagles from 1976–1982), the St. Louis Rams from 1997–1999 and the Kansas City Chiefs from 2001–2005. He has coached at every level. Vermeil owns the distinction of being named "Coach of the Year" on four levels: High School, Junior College, NCAA Division I and Professional Football.
In all three of his stops as an NFL head coach, Vermeil has taken every team, Philadelphia, St. Louis and Kansas City, each of

which had a losing record before he arrived and brought them to the playoffs by his third season at the helm.

The difference between the impossible and the possible lies in a man's determination. *~Tommy Lasorda*

Thomas Charles Lasorda is a former MLB baseball player that has had a lengthy career in sports management. In 2009 he had started his 6th decade with the Los Angeles Dodgers in some capacity or another passing Vin Scully by a single season. He had a career winning percentage of .526 in the regular season as a manager and a .508 win percentage in the post season. He was inducted into the MLB Hall of Fame as a manager in 1997.

Famous quotes that stand the test of time are those that have relevance. Quotes can be useful nuggets of information. A captured wisdom. I wanted to do something creative with some of the quotes I came across and present them in an original manner. Sort of a Fun with Quotes. All quotes are actual quotes from those listed in this book. Any quotes listed without someone by name quoting them are anonymous quotes. The manner in which the quotes are presented is completely fictional and is simply meant for enjoyment.

And I Quote.... ANGER & HATE

"Anger is an acid that can do more harm to the vessel in which it is stored than to anything on which it is poured" Mark Twain spoke into the microphone.

Coretta Scott King patted Mark on the back, took the microphone, and faced the crowd.
"Hate is too great a burden to bear. It injures the hater more than it injures the hated."

Buddha joined them up on the stage. Buddha needed no microphone. His soothing voice traveled on the wind through the crowd.
"Holding on to anger is like grasping a hot coal with the intent of throwing it at someone else; you are the one who gets burned."

Will Smith grabbed the microphone, gave Buddha a fist pump, gave Buddha's belly a rub and stated. **"Throughout life people will make you mad, disrespect you and treat you bad. Let God deal with the things they do, cause hate in your heart will consume you too."** He looked back at Buddha and winked.

And I Quote.... DISCIPLINE & ACTION

Jim Rohn spoke to the group there in the studio

"Discipline is the bridge between goals & accomplishment."

David Campbell scratched his head and lectured
"Discipline is remembering what you want"

Vaclav Havel pointed in the direction of the two men in an authoritative fashion
"Vision is not enough, it must be combined with venture. It is not enough to stare up the steps, we must step up the stairs."

Pablo Picasso stroked his final touches to painting, rolling his eyes at the other three
"Action is the foundational key to all success."

And I Quote.... EXPERIENCE

The subject was experience and the wise sat in a circle discussing the topic.
James Russell Lowell cleared his throat and offered
"One thorn of experience is worth a whole wilderness of warning."
The others clapped in approval.
Oliver Wendell Holmes Jr. stood up and added
"A mind that is stretched by a new experience can never go back to its old dimensions."
Another round of applause came from those present as he returned to his seat.
At that time Albert Einstein theorized
"The only source of knowledge is experience"
A round of applause echoed again.
Next, Oscar Wilde noted
"Experience is simply the name we give our mistakes"
yet another round of applause, at that time Rita Mae Brown leaned over and French kissed the woman next to her met by awkward stares from those present
"Good judgement comes from experience, and experience comes

from bad judgement" She smiled heartily back at them.

And I Quote.... STRATEGY & RISK

Jef Richards walked into the room sporting his Adidas Cap & tee, straightened his Adidas Jacket and approached the podium
"Creativity without strategy is called 'Art.' Creative with strategy is called advertising"

The crowd filled with many Nike employees booed & hissed 'Just do it'. Rob Manuel entered the room took his place behind the podium, hushed the crowd and started with a whisper
"There's a certain logic to avoiding the haters, but as a strategy it's utterly flawed. When you turn off the feedback, you lose the benefits as well as the drawbacks. It's like having a sore finger & cutting off your arm"

Winston Churchhill took in the commotion and eventual silence, stood up and headed towards the podium and preached
"However beautiful the strategy, you should occasionally look at the results"

The silence remained. A voice came from the back of the auditorium. Sitting there in a brown tweed jacket was Michael Porter, he stood and said **"The essence of strategy is choosing what not to do."**

Mark Zuckerberg,a row behind Michael tapped him on the back
"The biggest risk is not taking any risk.... In a world that's changing really quickly, the only strategy that is guaranteed to fail is not taking the risks"

Muhammad Ali sat next to Michael Porter and took in Zuckerberg's words nodding in agreement
"He who is not courageous enough to take risks will accomplish nothing in life."

Edward Whitacre Jr burst in from the rear streaked his way up to the podium in his birthday suit to everyone's dismay

"Be willing to step outside your comfort zone once in a while; take the risks in life that seem worth taking. The ride might not be as predictable if you'd just planted your feet and stayed put, but it will be a heck of a lot more interesting"

And I Quote…. COFFEE, TEA, AND A BIT OF CAFFEINE

The coffee lovers of America convention was held in Reno, NV. There was an open group conversation going on where you would state something coffee related. Various known & unknown coffee enthusiasts were gathered around in a circle. A man in a green jacket spoke up **"Herbal tea tastes so much better when it's coffee"**
A witty gentleman a couple rows deep spouted
"Deja Brew: The feeling that you've had this coffee before"
A woman wearing a red flower patterned dress gave
"Chocolate, men, coffee – some things are better rich"
The man next to her responded
"I like my coffee like my women: hot, strong, … and steamy"
He finished with a wink back at the woman.
A heavy set man bellowed
"Decaffeinated coffee is the devil's blend"
Nearby a young fellow wearing a derby continued
"A yawn is a silent scream for coffee"
Another young man stated
"Coffee is a hug in a mug"
Terri Guillemets stood on her chair
"Coffee makes me invincible. But when the cup is empty, I return to mere mortal"
She then finished her cup of java and slinked back to ground level.
At this time the tea lovers convention held the next room over had let out and a few of the tea lovers had made their way into the fray. An English bloke blurted out"**Bread and water can so easily be toast and tea**"
A silent hush hit the crowd when another tea enthusiast spat out **"Tea

is a cup of life"

Terri Guillemets stood back on her chair **"The perfect temperature for tea is two degrees hotter than just right"**

Murmurs of traitor were heard before another boasted **"Tea is liquid wisdom"**

Samuel Goldwyn drew the final straw and had the two conventions at each others throats when he grabbed the conference room microphone and said with a mocking grin **"Coffee is not my cup of tea"**

At this point a referee had to step in to bring peace and order to the crowd.

Abraham Lincoln coaxed the microphone off of Samuel Goldwyn and spewed forth a peaceful logic

"If this is coffee, bring me some tea; but if this is tea, please bring me some coffee"

This seemed to calm the opposing parties when another peacemaker stepped forth

"Caffeine isn't a drug, it's a vitamin"

All in the room cheered. Bill Ayers raised his hand to garner attention **"I have an addiction to caffeine"**

More cheers from the convention room. Eddie Vedder in a relaxed manner pointed over to Bill Ayers and said **"Caffeine. The gateway drug"** Chuckles arose along with laughs. Everyone in the room was now relaxed and in good spirits as they sipped their beverages of choice and went about their merry way.

And I quote…. COMPLAINTS

They both read through the pile of letters, when another pile was dumped on their desks Mason Cooley spoke

"complainers change their complaints, but they never reduce the amount of time spent in complaining"

Ben Franklin looked over at Mason

"Any fool can criticize, condemn and complain – And most fools do!"

And I Quote…. QUOTES

After reading the book 'And I Quote' by Robert McGinley Hazrat Ali said to the critics

"Like your body your mind also gets tired so refresh it by wise sayings"

Abraham Lincoln read the book through twice, chuckling over multiple entries

"It is a pleasure to be able to quote lines to fit any occasion."

Rudyard Kipling tossed his Kindle aside after finishing the last chapter

"He wrapped himself in quotations- as a beggar would enfold himself in the purple of emperors"

Robert Brault picked up the discarded Kindle, sat down, got a little past midway of the material

"I'm discovering that everybody is a closet quotesmith. Just give them a chance."

Robert M Hamilton got to the last page of his paperback, turning over the outside cover of the book, looking for more **"A book of quotations…. Can never be complete"**